Family Violence

Other Books in the Current Controversies Series

Current
CONTROVERSIES

Family Violence

Nancy Dziedzic, Book Editor

GREENHAVEN PRESS
A part of Gale, Cengage Learning

GALE
CENGAGE Learning

Detroit • New York • San Francisco • New Haven, Conn • Waterville, Maine • London

Christine Nasso, *Publisher*
Elizabeth Des Chenes, *Managing Editor*

© 2009 Greenhaven Press, a part of Gale, Cengage Learning

Gale and Greenhaven Press are registered trademarks used herein under license.

For more information, contact:
Greenhaven Press
27500 Drake Rd.
Farmington Hills, MI 48331-3535
Or you can visit our Internet site at gale.cengage.com

For product information and technology assistance, contact us at

Gale Customer Support, 1-800-877-4253
For permission to use material from this text or product, submit all requests online at
www.cengage.com/permissions

Further permissions questions can be emailed to permissionrequest@cengage.com

Articles in Greenhaven Press anthologies are often edited for length to meet page requirements. In addition, original titles of these works are changed to clearly present the main thesis and to explicitly indicate the author's opinion. Every effort is made to ensure that Greenhaven Press accurately reflects the original intent of the authors. Every effort has been made to trace the owners of copyrighted material.

Cover image © Tom and Dee Ann McCarthy/Corbis.

LIBRARY OF CONGRESS CATALOGING-IN-PUBLICATION DATA

Family violence / Nancy Dziedzic, book editor.
    p. cm. -- (Current controversies)
    Includes bibliographical references and index.
    ISBN-13: 978-0-7377-3283-2 (hardcover)
    ISBN-13: 978-0-7377-3284-9 (pbk.)
    1. Family violence. 2. Family violence--Prevention. I. Dziedzic, Nancy G.
    HV6626.F33 2009
    362.82'92--dc22
                                                2008047459

Printed in the United States of America
1 2 3 4 5 6 7 13 12 11 10 09

Contents

Chapter 1: What Is the Scope of Family Violence?

Rana Sampson

Violence between intimate partners not only affects the
physical and psychological well-being of victims and
their children but also impacts the larger workforce and
economy as victims may be unable to maintain steady
employment and may become dependent on publicly
funded social welfare programs. Numerous theories exist
to explain why some men and women become batterers,
as well as why victims so often are reluctant to leave
their abusers.

*Children's Bureau, U.S. Department of Health
and Human Services, Administration on Children,
Youth, and Families*

Abuse of children in the home can include neglect of
basic needs, physical violence, sexual abuse, emotional or
psychological mistreatment, and withholding of medical
care. Perpetrators of family violence against children
most often are parents, with mothers under the age of
thirty the most likely to commit child abuse.

Chapter 2: What Contributes to Family Violence?

Chapter 3: Is Domestic Violence a Gender Issue?

Yes: Efforts to Reduce Family Violence Are Effective

No: Efforts to Reduce Family Violence Are Not Effective

Foreword

By definition, controversies are "discussions of questions in which opposing opinions clash" (*Webster's Twentieth Century Dictionary Unabridged*). Few would deny that controversies are a pervasive part of the human condition and exist on virtually every level of human enterprise. Controversies transpire between individuals and among groups, within nations and between nations. Controversies supply the grist necessary for progress by providing challenges and challengers to the status quo. They also create atmospheres where strife and warfare can flourish. A world without controversies would be a peaceful world; but it also would be, by and large, static and prosaic.

The Series' Purpose

The purpose of the *Current Controversies* series is to explore many of the social, political, and economic controversies dominating the national and international scenes today. Titles selected for inclusion in the series are highly focused and specific. For example, from the larger category of criminal justice, *Current Controversies* deals with specific topics such as police brutality, gun control, white collar crime, and others. The debates in *Current Controversies* also are presented in a useful, timeless fashion. Articles and book excerpts included in each title are selected if they contribute valuable, long-range ideas to the overall debate. And wherever possible, current information is enhanced with historical documents and other relevant materials. Thus, while individual titles are current in focus, every effort is made to ensure that they will not become quickly outdated. Books in the *Current Controversies* series will remain important resources for librarians, teachers, and students for many years.

In addition to keeping the titles focused and specific, great care is taken in the editorial format of each book in the series. Book introductions and chapter prefaces are offered to provide background material for readers. Chapters are organized around several key questions that are answered with diverse opinions representing all points on the political spectrum. Materials in each chapter include opinions in which authors clearly disagree as well as alternative opinions in which authors may agree on a broader issue but disagree on the possible solutions. In this way, the content of each volume in *Current Controversies* mirrors the mosaic of opinions encountered in society. Readers will quickly realize that there are many viable answers to these complex issues. By questioning each author's conclusions, students and casual readers can begin to develop the critical thinking skills so important to evaluating opinionated material.

Current Controversies is also ideal for controlled research. Each anthology in the series is composed of primary sources taken from a wide gamut of informational categories including periodicals, newspapers, books, U.S. and foreign government documents, and the publications of private and public organizations. Readers will find factual support for reports, debates, and research papers covering all areas of important issues. In addition, an annotated table of contents, an index, a book and periodical bibliography, and a list of organizations to contact are included in each book to expedite further research.

Perhaps more than ever before in history, people are confronted with diverse and contradictory information. During the Persian Gulf War, for example, the public was not only treated to minute-to-minute coverage of the war, it was also inundated with critiques of the coverage and countless analyses of the factors motivating U.S. involvement. Being able to sort through the plethora of opinions accompanying today's major issues, and to draw one's own conclusions, can be a complicated and frustrating struggle. It is the editors' hope that *Current Controversies* will help readers with this struggle.

Introduction

"Although the social, cultural, and finan-
cial circumstances of victims and perpe-
trators may differ, and some forms of
family violence may seem more shocking
or disturbing than others, the effects of-
ten are the same: families' lives are shat-
tered, children fail to thrive, and even
economies can suffer.

Family violence, also commonly known as domestic violence, knows no bounds; it is an international problem
that exists in one form or another in every country on the
planet. In its June 2000 publication, *Domestic Violence Against
Women and Girls*, the United Nations Children's Fund
(UNICEF) reported that 28 percent of women in the United
States, 41 percent of women in Uganda, 35 percent of women
in Egypt, and 38 percent of women in Korea acknowledged
they had been physically or sexually abused by their partners.
In the Indian state of Uttar Pradesh, 45 percent of married
men surveyed admitted they had beaten their wives. In all, an
estimated 10 to 50 percent of women worldwide are battered.

UNICEF's definition of domestic violence includes physical abuse, sexual abuse and intimate-partner rape, psychological and emotional abuse, spousal homicide, sexual abuse of
children and teenagers, forced prostitution, abortion of female
fetuses and infanticide of female children, and unequal access
to food and medical care.

Domestic violence also can include traditional social practices, such as female genital mutilation (also called female cir-
cumcision, this is the practice of surgically removing, usually
without anesthesia, all or part of the external female genitalia
for cultural or religious reasons), honor killings, and dowry

violence, that adversely affect women's and girls' lives and health. While some of these acts of domestic violence are universal, others occur more frequently in cultures where male social, religious, and political dominance is more extreme, poverty more widespread and severe, and women's rights virtually unheard of.

Culturally specific forms of domestic violence are some of the most misunderstood and controversial because they so often are based on historical precedents related to religious tradition. Proponents of multiculturalism may defend a practice such as female genital mutilation because it is uniquely tied to non-Western religious custom. Such proponents may argue that to impose Western moral judgment on other cultures is unfair and hypocritical. On the other hand, groups such as Amnesty International and the World Health Organization have adopted a zero-tolerance approach to female genital mutilation, believing that its damage to women and girls extends beyond even the scope of the term "domestic violence"—it is, rather, a fundamental violation of human rights that must be globally eradicated.

Honor killings—in which a girl or woman is murdered by male relatives or their associates because she has allegedly shamed the family by dating a boy outside her religion, getting pregnant outside of marriage, or even being raped or cooking a less-than-perfect meal—are similarly controversial. While honor killings are perpetrated most often in parts of Asia and the Middle East, there have been highly publicized cases in Europe, Great Britain, and the United States since 2000, and they are believed to occur in other societies where notions of family honor and shame are strong. Because honor killings are considered justifiable in some communities, they rarely are reported to authorities, and local police are reluctant to pursue those cases that are reported. Honor killings commonly are associated in the public's mind with the Muslim faith, but such incidents occur in a variety of cultures, as explained by the BBC News: "Honor killings are much more about male-dominated societies or communities that try to stop women making their own decisions. In other words, the killers believe it is culturally acceptable for them to murder to preserve, in their mind, the good name of the family."

In India and other Southeast Asian countries, the families of young women often are expected to give money and goods to their grooms' families. This dowry system was officially outlawed in India in 1961, but the practice continues and has, in fact, become more dangerous in recent years for young brides. Some families who cannot or will not continue to meet the demands of their in-laws for increasingly costly items—including gold, cars, and houses—are violently harassed. In 2005 nearly 7,000 women were murdered or committed suicide because their families could not or would not continue to pay their husbands' or fiances' families. The most common way for grooms or their family members to kill the women is by pouring kerosene over them and setting them on fire. Sometimes, desperate to stop the constant harassment, women kill themselves in this way. "Bride burning," as it has come to be known, became such a widespread problem in India that the country passed the Protection of Women from Domestic Violence Act in 2006. The legislation has not ended dowry violence, but the incidence has decreased slightly since its passage.

The United Nations Population Fund (UNFPA) estimates that 113 to 200 million girls and women are "missing" from the global population—in other words, statistical trends dictate that there should be hundreds of millions more females in the world than there are. There is no record of their deaths, or even of their births. So where are those girls and women? Ayaan Hirsi Ali, a Somali-born legislator in The Netherlands, blames family violence: sex-selective abortions, infanticide of female babies, honor killings, dowry murders, sex-trade-related deaths, neglect due to the withholding of food and medical treatment to female children, and deaths due to complications from female genital mutilation and acid attacks together add up to untold numbers of deaths of girls and women worldwide, many of which go unreported. "What is happening to women and girls in many places across the globe is genocide," Hirsi Ali asserts.

These numbers do not take into account the millions of other people—mostly in wealthier, industrialized nations—who are affected by family violence. Children, spouses, elderly relatives, siblings, and even family pets can be caught in the cycle of violence. Although social, cultural, and financial circumstances of victims and perpetrators may differ, and some forms of family violence may seem more shocking or disturbing than others, the effects often are the same: victims' lives are shattered, children fail to thrive, and even economies can suffer.

This book explores family violence primarily in the Western cultural context. Chapter 1, "What Is the Scope of Family Violence?" examines the many different victims of domestic violence in the United States. Other chapters include "What Contributes to Family Violence?," "Is Domestic Violence a Gender Issue?," and "Are Efforts to Reduce Family Violence Effective?" The viewpoints explored in *Current Controversies: Family Violence* will help readers understand the ongoing debates surrounding this urgent social problem.

What Is the Scope of Family Violence?

Chapter Preface

In the United States, family violence occurs in every demographic group. Rich and poor, young and old, male and female—anyone could be a victim; anyone could be a perpetrator. Because family violence is such a complex criminal and psychological act, with victims caught in and perpetrators engaged in the cycle of abuse, it is typically one of the most secretive of crimes. Ashamed of what they see as their own weakness, terrified of their batterers and at the same time wanting to protect them, victims tend to be reluctant to speak up. Often it is outside observers—friends, neighbors, coworkers, teachers—who sense a problem.

In general, habitual abusers rely on several tactics, including dominance, humiliation, isolation, threats, intimidation, denial, and blame, to coerce their victims into remaining in the relationship and not seeking help. Obedience and control are the hallmarks of family violence. In order to maintain control of a spouse, child, or parent, a batterer will demand absolute obedience from family members, who are expected to ask permission to perform the simplest acts. Victims are called names, insulted, and made fun of in front of others to break down their self-esteem and induce them to stay. Victims are discouraged or even prevented from seeing friends and family. An atmosphere of terror may pervade the household, with abusers destroying objects, harming pets, brandishing weapons, and, ultimately, blaming their victims for the battering. Financial control is another key element of family violence, especially in the case of elderly and disabled victims, who also may be improperly medicated by abusers.

The cycle of violence follows an established pattern. According to Helpguide, a nonprofit health organization based in Santa Monica, California, the cycle begins with the abuser committing an act of violence against his or her victim. Fear-ing being found out and having to face consequences, as well as, in many cases, experiencing guilt, the abuser begins to rationalize the behavior. A "honeymoon" phase follows, during which batterers may be apologetic and charming; this ensures a victim will forgive and begin to believe things will change. In reality, however, the abuser has already moved on to fantasizing about his or her next act of abuse, having decided that the victim cannot be trusted and deserves punishment. This is the pattern when abusers exhibit paranoia and obsess about their partners betraying them, which in turn leads to the next outburst of violence.

The selections in this chapter analyze the widespread incidence of family violence, discussing victims who are targeted directly as well as incidental victims. The authors examine the numbers of men, women, children, parents, and animals who suffer silently in the United States, and also explore the patterns that emerge across groups of batterers and victims.

An Overview of Intimate Partner Violence

Rana Sampson

Rana Sampson is a crime consultant at the Center for Problem-Oriented Policing in San Diego. An attorney and former officer with the New York City Police Department, she has published many articles and manuals on violent crime, including domestic violence.

Domestic violence involves a current or former intimate (and in many states, a current or former dating partner). Domestic violence tends to be underreported: women report only one-quarter to one-half of their assaults to police, men perhaps less. The vast majority of physical assaults are not life threatening; rather, they involve pushing, slapping, and hitting. Most women victims of domestic violence do not seek medical treatment, even for injuries deserving of it.

Surveys Offer Varied Data

Surveys provide us with estimates of the level of domestic violence in the United States, but there are wide differences among them depending on the definitions of domestic violence used and populations surveyed. Two large surveys provide some insight into the level of domestic violence in the United States. The first, the National Violence Against Women Survey (NVAWS), conducted in 1995 and 1996, found that nearly one in four women and nearly one in 13 men surveyed experienced rape and/or physical assault by a current or former spouse/partner/dating partner at some time in their lifetime, with about one and one-half percent of women and about one percent of men having been so victimized in the 12

Rana Sampson, *Domestic Violence*, Problem-Oriented Guides for Police, Problem-Specific Guides Series, no. 45. U.S. Department of Justice Office of Community Oriented Policing Services, 2007. *www.cops.usdoj.gov.*

months before the survey. The National Crime Victimization Survey's (NCVS) estimates, however, are about one-third lower for women and more than two-thirds lower for men. Differences in survey administration and methodology may account for the large differences in the numbers.

Even the lower numbers of the NCVS suggest that intimate partner violence in the United States is extensive. However, NCVS trend data through 2001 show that partner violence between current and former intimates has declined significantly. From 1993 through 2001, the rate of reported intimate violence dropped by about 50 percent in the United States. From 1994 through 2001, the rate of every major violent and property crime declined by similar percentages. It is unknown whether domestic violence is paralleling these declines for the same or different reasons.

There is a robust debate among researchers about the level of relationship violence women are responsible for and the extent to which it is in self-defense or fighting back.

Domestic violence homicides have declined in similar proportions as well. In the United States, there were about half the number of intimate partner homicides (spouses, ex-spouses, boyfriends, and girlfriends) in 2002 as there were in 1976, with the largest portion of the decline in male victims.

Some commentators suggest that the decline in homicides may be evidence that abused women have developed legitimate ways to leave their relationships (e.g., divorce, shelters, police, and courts). The reasons for the decline may be even more complex because there is wide variation by race, not just by gender. Between 1976 and 2002, the number of black male victims of intimate partner homicide fell by 81 percent as compared to 56 percent for white males. The number of black female victims of intimate partner homicide fell 49 percent as compared to 9 percent for white females.

Women as Offenders

There is a robust debate among researchers about the level of relationship violence women are responsible for and the extent to which it is in self-defense or fighting back. The NCVS and other studies have found that women are the victims in as much as 85 percent of domestic violence incidents. However, there are also research findings that women in heterosexual relationships have the same, if not higher, rates of relationship violence as men. Generally, studies about domestic violence fall into two categories: family conflict studies and crime victimization studies. Those that tend to show high rates of violence by women (or rates higher than men) are family conflict studies and contain questions about family conflicts and disputes and responses to these, including physical responses. These studies use a family conflict assessment tool. Those studies that show that male assaultive behavior predominates in domestic violence are criminal victimization surveys and/or studies that rely on the counting of crime reports.

Batterers frequently also subject their victims to harassment (such as annoying or threatening phone calls), vandalism, trespassing, stalking, criminal mischief, theft, and burglary.

Critics suggest that studies finding about equal rates of violence by women in relationships are misleading because they fail to place the violence in context; in other words, there is a difference between someone who uses violence to fight back or defend oneself and someone who initiates an unprovoked assault. Also, the physical differences between some women and their male partners may make comparisons between equivalent types of violence (slapping, kicking, punching, hitting) less meaningful, particularly because many studies show that violence by women is less likely to result in injury. Researchers agree that women suffer the lion's share of injuries from domestic violence.

Women living as partners with other women report lower rates of violence (11 percent) compared to women who live with or were married to men (30 percent). About 8 percent of men living with or married to women report that they were physically abused by the women. About 15 percent of men cohabitating with men reported victimization by a male partner. These data suggest that men are engaged in more relationship violence.

Harms Caused by Domestic Violence

Domestic violence can include murder, rape, sexual assault, robbery, and aggravated or simple assault. In addition to the physical harm victims suffer, domestic violence results in emotional harm to victims, their children, other family members, friends, neighbors, and co-workers. Victims and their children experience the brunt of the psychological trauma of abuse, suffering anxiety, stress, sleep deprivation, loss of confidence, social isolation, and fear. Batterers frequently also subject their victims to harassment (such as annoying or threatening phone calls), vandalism, trespassing, stalking, criminal mischief, theft, and burglary.

Domestic violence also has economic costs. Victims may lose their jobs because of absenteeism related to the violence, and may even lose their homes because of loss of income. Some domestic violence victims must rely on shelters or depend on others to house them, and others become part of a community's homeless population, increasing their risk for other types of victimization. Medical expenses to treat injuries, particularly of uninsured victims, create additional financial burdens, either for the victims or for the public. . . .

Why Some Men Batter

Generally, four theories explain battering in intimate relationships.

Psychological theory. Battering is the result of childhood abuse, a personality trait (such as the need to control), a personality disturbance (such as borderline personality), psychopathology (such as anti-social personality), or a psychological disorder or problem (such as post traumatic stress, poor impulse control, low self-esteem, or substance abuse).

Sociological theory. Sociological theories vary but usually contain some suggestion that intimate violence is the result of learned behavior. One sociological theory suggests that violence is learned within a family, and a partner-victim stays caught up in a cycle of violence and forgiveness. If the victim does not leave, the batterer views the violence as a way to produce positive results. Children of these family members may learn the behavior from their parents (boys may develop into batterers and girls may become battering victims). A different sociological theory suggests that lower income subcultures will show higher rates of intimate abuse, as violence may be a more acceptable form of settling disputes in such subcultures. A variant on this theory is that violence is inherent in all social systems and people with resources (financial, social contacts, prestige) use these to control family members, while those without resort to violence and threats to accomplish this goal.

Feminist or societal-structural theory. According to this theory, male intimates who use violence do so to control and limit the independence of women partners. Societal traditions of male dominance support and sustain inequities in relationships.

Violent individuals theory. For many years it was assumed that domestic batterers were a special group, that while they assaulted their current or former intimates they were not violent in the outside world. There is cause to question how fully this describes batterers. Although the full extent of violence batterers perpetrate is unknown, there is evidence that many batterers are violent beyond domestic violence, and many have prior criminal records for violent and non-violent behavior. This suggests that domestic violence batterers are less unique and are more accurately viewed as violent criminals, not solely as domestic batterers. There may be a group of batterers who are violent only to their current or former intimates and engage in no other violent and non-violent criminal behavior, but this group may be small compared to the more common type of batterer.

Why Some Women Batter

Some women batter their current or former intimates. Less is known about women who use violence in relationships, particularly the extent to which it may be in self-defense, to fight back, or to ward off anticipated violence. When asked in a national survey if they used violence in their relationships, many Canadian college women said they did. However, the majority of these women said it was in self-defense or to fight back and that the more they were victimized the more they fought back. One researcher suggests that women should be discouraged from engaging in minor violence because it places them at risk for retaliation from men and men are more likely to be able to inflict injury.

Although many women do leave physically abusive relationships, others remain even after police intervene.

Clearly, there are women who use violence in relationships provocatively outside the context of fighting back or self-defense. The extent of this problem, as we noted earlier, remains unknown but is ripe for additional study.

The theories explaining male violence cited earlier may also have some relevance for women, although the picture is not clear.

Why Some Women Are Reluctant to End Abusive Relationships

Police commonly express frustration that many of the battered women they deal with do not leave their batterers. Although many women do leave physically abusive relationships, others remain even after police intervene. There is no reliable information about the percentage of women who stay in physically abusive relationships. Researchers offer a number of explanations for the resistance by some to leave an abuser.

Cycle of violence. Three cyclical phases in physically abusive intimate relationships keep a woman in the relationship: 1) a tension-building phase that includes minor physical and verbal abuse, 2) an acute battering phase, and 3) a makeup or honeymoon phase. The honeymoon phase lulls an abused woman into staying and the cycle repeats itself.

Battered woman syndrome. A woman is so fearful from experiencing cycles of violence that she no longer believes escape is possible.

Stockholm syndrome. A battered woman is essentially a hostage to her batterer. She develops a bond with and shows support for and kindness to her captor, perhaps because of her isolation from and deprivation of more normal relationships.

Traumatic bonding theory. A battered woman experienced unhealthy or anxious attachments to her parents who abused or neglected her. The woman develops unhealthy attachments in her adult relationships and accepts intermittent violence from her intimate partner. She believes the affection and claims of remorse that follow because she needs positive acceptance from and bonding with the batterer.

Psychological entrapment theory. A woman feels she has invested so much in the relationship, she is willing to tolerate the battering to save it.

Although domestic violence occurs across income brackets, it is most frequently reported by the poor, who more often rely on the police for dispute resolution.

Multifactor ecological perspective. Staying in physically abusive relationships is the result of a combination of factors, including family history, personal relationships, societal norms, and social and cultural factors. . . .

Factors Contributing to Domestic Violence

Risk factors do not automatically mean that a person will become a domestic violence victim or an offender. Also, although some risk factors are stronger than others, it is difficult to compare risk factor findings across studies because of methodological differences between studies.

Age. The female age group at highest risk for domestic violence victimization is 16 to 24. Among one segment of this high-risk age group—undergraduate college students—22 percent of female respondents in a Canadian study reported domestic violence victimization, and 14 percent of male respondents reported physically assaulting their dating partners in the year before the survey. And although the victimization of teen girls is estimated to be high, it is difficult to ". . . untangle defensive responses from acts of initial violence against a dating partner" [as written by Laura Hickman, Lisa Jaycox, and Jessica Aronoff].

Socioeconomic status. Although domestic violence occurs across income brackets, it is most frequently reported by the poor, who more often rely on the police for dispute resolution. Victimization surveys indicate that lower-income women are, in fact, more frequently victims of domestic violence than wealthier women. Women with family income less than $7,500 are five times more likely to be victims of violence by an intimate than women with family annual incomes between $50,000 and $74,000.

Although the poorest women are the most victimized by domestic violence, one study also found that women receiving government income support payments through Aid for Families with Dependent Children (AFDC) were three times more likely to have experienced physical aggression by a current or former partner during the previous year than non-AFDC supported women.

Race. Overall, in the United States, blacks experience higher rates of victimization than other groups: black females experience intimate violence at a rate 35 percent higher than that of white females, and black males experience intimate violence at a rate about 69 percent higher than that of white males and about two and a half times the rate of men of other races. Other survey research, more inclusive of additional racial groups, finds that American Indian/Alaskan Native women experience significantly higher rates of physical abuse as well.

Many of those convicted of domestic violence have a prior conviction history: more than 70 percent of offenders in jail for domestic violence have prior convictions for other crimes.

Repeat victimization. Domestic violence, generally, has high levels of repeat calls for police service. For instance, police data in West Yorkshire (United Kingdom) showed that 42 percent of domestic violence incidents within one year were repeat offenses, and one-third of domestic violence offenders were responsible for two-thirds of all domestic violence incidents reported to the police. It is likely that some victims of domestic violence experience physical assault only once and others experience it repeatedly over a period as short as 12 months. British research suggests that the highest risk period for further assault is within the first four weeks of the last assault.

Incarceration of offenders. Offenders convicted of domestic violence account for about 25 percent of violent offenders in local jails and 7 percent of violent offenders in state prisons. Many of those convicted of domestic violence have a prior conviction history: more than 70 percent of offenders in jail for domestic violence have prior convictions for other crimes, not necessarily domestic violence.

Termination of the relationship. Although there is a popular conception that the risk of domestic violence increases when a couple separates, in fact, most assaults occur during a relationship rather than after it is over. However, still unknown is whether the severity (as opposed to the frequency) of violence increases once a battered woman leaves.

Pregnancy. Contrary to popular belief, pregnant women are no more likely than non-pregnant women to be victims of domestic violence. In fact, some women get a reprieve from violence during pregnancy. The risk of abuse during pregnancy is greatest for women who experienced physical abuse before the pregnancy. Some additional factors increase the risk during pregnancy: being young and poor and if the pregnancy was unintended. Physical abuse during the pregnancy can result in pre-term delivery, low birth weight, birth defects, miscarriage, and fetal death.

Multiple risk factors for women and men. Being young, black, low-income, divorced or separated, a resident of rental housing, and a resident of an urban area have all been associated with higher rates of domestic violence victimization among women. For male victims, the patterns were nearly identical: being young, black, divorced or separated, or a resident of rental housing. In New Zealand, a highly respected study found that the strongest predictor for committing partner violence among the many risk factors in childhood and adolescence is a history of aggressive delinquency before age 15.

There is a strong link between threat of bodily injury and actual bodily injury, suggesting that abuser threats should be taken seriously.

The study also found that committing partner violence is strongly linked to cohabitation at a young age; a variety of mental illnesses; a background of family adversity; dropping out of school; juvenile aggression; conviction for other types of crime, especially violent crime; drug abuse; long-term unemployment; and parenthood at a young age.

Other risk factors. Several other risk factors emerge from research:

- A verbally abusive partner is one of the most robust risk factors for intimate partner violence.

- Women whose partners are jealous or tightly controlling are at increased risk of intimate violence and stalking.

- There is a strong link between threat of bodily injury and actual bodily injury, suggesting that abuser threats should be taken seriously.

Recently, there is much discussion among police about the link between pet abuse and domestic violence. Although some overlap is likely, particularly under the theory that many batterers are generally violent, not enough is known because of the types of studies undertaken. Some small surveys of domestic violence shelter residents suggest that some women might have left their abuser sooner but they worried about their pet's safety.

Finally, although alcohol and drug use do not cause intimate partner battering, the risk of victim injury increases if a batterer is using alcohol or drugs.

Children Can Be Victims of Family Violence

Children's Bureau, U.S. Department of Health and Human Services, Administration on Children, Youth, and Families

The U.S. Department of Health and Human Services Administration on Children, Youth, and Families runs federal programs that help to empower American families by promoting their social and economic well-being.

Each State has its own definitions of child abuse and neglect based on minimum standards set by Federal law. Federal legislation provides a foundation for States by identifying a minimum set of acts or behaviors that defines child abuse and neglect. The Federal Child Abuse Prevention and Treatment Act (CAPTA), as amended by the Keeping Children and Families Safe Act of 2003, defines child abuse and neglect as, at minimum:

- Any recent act or failure to act on the part of a parent or caretaker which results in death, serious physical or emotional harm, sexual abuse or exploitation; or

- An act or failure to act which presents an imminent risk of serious harm.

Child protective services (CPS) agencies respond to the needs of children who are alleged to have been maltreated and ensure that they are safe. National estimates for FFY 2005 are based on child populations for the 50 States, the District of Columbia, and Puerto Rico. FFY 2005 is the first year that Puerto Rico's data have been included in [the U.S. Department

Children's Bureau, U.S. Department of Health and Human Services, Administration on Children, Youth, and Families, *Child Maltreatment 2005*. Washington, DC: U.S. Government Printing Office, 2007. *www.acf.hhs.gov.*

of Health and Human Services' 2005 report,] *Child Maltreatment.* During Federal fiscal year (FFY) 2005:

- An estimated 899,000 children were victims of maltreatment;

- The rate of victimization was 12.1 per 1,000 children in the population; and

- Nearly 3.6 million children received a CPS investigation or assessment. . . .

Children Who Were Subjects of an Investigation

Based on a rate of 48.3 per 1,000 children, an estimated 3.6 million children received an investigation by CPS agencies during FFY 2005. The rate of all children who received an investigation or assessment increased from 43.2 per 1,000 children for 2001 to 48.3 per 1,000 children for FFY 2005. The increase of approximately 73,000 children who received an investigation in FFY 2005, compared to FFY 2004, is largely due to the inclusion of data from Alaska and Puerto Rico in FFY 2005. The national estimates are based upon counting a child each time he or she was the subject of a CPS investigation. Heightened public awareness of child maltreatment also may have played a factor.

Child victims. Of the children who received an investigation, approximately one-quarter were determined to have been abused or neglected. Based on a victim rate of 12.1 per 1,000 children, an estimated 899,000 children were found to be victims in the 50 states, the District of Columbia, and Puerto Rico. The increase of approximately 20,000 victims in FFY 2005, compared to FFY 2004, is largely due to the inclusion of data from Alaska and Puerto Rico. . . .

The rate of victimization decreased from 12.5 per 1,000 during 2001, to 12.1 per 1,000 children during FFY 2005, which is a 3.2 percent decrease (if data from Alaska and Puerto Rico were not included, the rate would be 12.0, or the same as FFY 2004.) State-specific 5-year trends illustrate similar proportions of States increased their rate as States decreased their rate.

The patterns of reporting of neglect and sexual abuse victims were similar—police officers or lawyers accounted for the largest report source percentage of neglect victims and the largest percentage of sexual abuse victims.

First-time victims. Three-quarters of victims (75.3%) had no history or prior victimization. Information regarding first-time victims is a Program Assessment Rating Tool (PART) measure. The Community-Based Child Abuse Prevention Program reports this PART measure to the Office of Management and Budget (OMB) each year as an average of all States. Individual State data are not reported to OMB.

Types of Maltreatment

During FFY 2005, 62.8 percent of victims experienced neglect, 16.6 percent were physically abused, 9.3 percent were sexually abused, 7.1 percent were psychologically maltreated, and 2.0 percent were medically neglected. In addition, 14.3 percent of victims experienced such "other" types of maltreatment as "abandonment," "threats of harm to the child," or "congenital drug addiction." States may code any condition that does not fall into one of the main categories—physical abuse, neglect, medical neglect, sexual abuse, and psychological or emotional maltreatment—as "other." These maltreatment type percentages total more than 100 percent because children who were victims of more than one type of maltreatment were counted for each maltreatment.

The data for victims of specific types of maltreatment were analyzed in terms of the report sources. Of victims of physical abuse, 24.3 percent were reported by teachers, 23.0

percent were reported by police officers or lawyers, and 11.6 percent were reported by medical staff. Overall, 74.8 percent were reported by professionals and 25.2 percent were reported by nonprofessionals. The patterns of reporting of neglect and sexual abuse victims were similar—police officers or lawyers accounted for the largest report source percentage of neglect victims (26.6%) and the largest percentage of sexual abuse victims (28.3%).

Sex and Age of Victims

For FFY 2005, 47.3 percent of child victims were boys, and 50.7 percent of the victims were girls. The youngest children had the highest rate of victimization. The rate of child victimization for the age group of birth to 3 years was 16.5 per 1,000 children of the same age group. The victimization rate for children in the age group of 4–7 years was 13.5 per 1,000 children in the same age group. Overall, the rate of victimization was inversely related to the age group of the child.

Nearly three-quarters of child victims (73.1%) ages birth to 3 years were neglected compared with 52.7 percent of victims ages 16 years and older. For victims in the age group of 4–7 years, 15.6 percent were physically abused and 8.9 percent were sexually abused, compared with 21.3 percent and 17.3 percent, respectively, for victims in the age group of 12–15 years old.

Race and Ethnicity of Victims

African-American children, American Indian or Alaska Native children, and Pacific Islander children had the highest rates of victimization at 19.5, 16.5, and 16.1 per 1,000 children of the same race or ethnicity, respectively. White children and Hispanic children had rates of approximately 10.8 and 10.7 per 1,000 children of the same race or ethnicity, respectively. Asian children had the lowest rate of 2.5 per 1,000 children of the same race or ethnicity.

Living Arrangement of Victims

Data are incomplete for the living arrangement of victims. Only one-half of the States were able to report on living arrangement and among these States, nearly 40 percent of the victims (37.2%) had unknown or missing data on living arrangement. Approximately 12 percent of victims (12.2%) were reported as living with married parents or married parent and stepparent. Approximately 13 percent (13.4%) of victims were living with both parents, but the marital status of the parents was unknown. More than 20 percent (23.0%) were living with a single parent. Less than 3 percent (2.9%) were reported as living with unmarried parents. It is hoped that reporting will improve in the coming years.

Reported Disability of Victims

Children who were reported with the following risk factors were considered as having a disability: mental retardation, emotional disturbance, visual or hearing impairment, learning disability, physical disability, behavioral problems, or another medical problem. In general, children with such risk factors are undercounted, as not every child receives a clinical diagnostic assessment from CPS agency staff. Nearly 8 percent (7.7%) of victims had a reported disability. More than 3 percent (3.2%) of victims had behavior problems and 1.9 percent of victims were emotionally disturbed. A victim could have been reported with more than one type of disability.

Recurrence

For many victims who have experienced repeat maltreatment, the efforts of the CPS system have not been successful in preventing subsequent victimization. Through the Child and Family Services Reviews (CFSR), the Children's Bureau has established the current national standard for recurrence as 94.6 percent, defined as:

Absence of Maltreatment Recurrence. Of all children who were victims of substantiated or indicated abuse or neglect during the first 6 months of the reporting year, what percent did not experience another incident of substantiated or indicated abuse or neglect within a 6-month period?. . .

Perpetrators of Maltreatment

Nearly 84 percent (83.4%) of victims were abused by a parent acting alone or with another person. Approximately forty percent (40.4%) of child victims were maltreated by their mothers acting alone; another 18.3 percent were maltreated by their fathers acting alone; and 17.3 percent were abused by both parents. Victims abused by nonparental perpetrators accounted for 10.7 percent. A nonparental perpetrator is defined as a caregiver who is not a parent and can include foster parent, child daycare staff, unmarried partner of parent, legal guardian, and residential facility staff.

More than three-quarters of children who were killed [due to maltreatment] were younger than four years of age.

The data for victims of specific maltreatment types were analyzed in terms of perpetrator relationship to the victim. Of the victims who experienced neglect, 86.6 percent were neglected by a parent. Of the victims who were sexually abused, 28.7 percent were abused by a relative other than a parent.

Maltreatment in Foster Care

Through the CFSR, the Children's Bureau established a national standard for the incidence of child abuse or neglect in foster care as 99.68 percent, defined as:

Absence of Maltreatment in Foster Care. Of all children in foster care during the reporting period, what percent were not victims of a substantiated or indicated maltreatment by foster parents or facility staff members?. . .

Fatalities Due to Child Maltreatment

Child fatalities are the most tragic consequence of maltreatment. The collection of accurate data regarding fatalities attributed to child abuse and neglect is challenging and requires coordination among many agencies. According to a recent article, "the ambiguity involved in investigation and determining the cause of a child's death often prevents accurate estimates of death from maltreatment." The NCANDS case-level data are from public child protective services (CPS) agencies and, therefore, do not include information for deaths that are not investigated by a CPS agency. Recognizing that the data from CPS agencies may be underestimated, NCANDS also recommends to States that they work with their health departments, vital statistics departments, medical examiners offices, and their fatality review teams to obtain information about other deaths and report these data in the Agency File. During Federal fiscal year (FFY) 2005:

- There were an estimated 1,460 child fatality victims;

- Approximately one-fifth (18.5%) of child fatality data were reported from agencies other than child welfare; and

- More than three-quarters (76.6%) of child fatality victims were younger than 4 years. . . .

Number and Characteristics of Child Fatalities

During FFY 2005, an estimated 1,460 children (compared to 1,490 children for FFY 2004) died from abuse or neglect—at a rate of 1.96 deaths per 100,000 children. The national estimate was based on data from State child welfare information systems, as well as other data sources available to the States. The rate of 1.96 is a decrease from the rate for FFY 2004 of 2.03 per 100,000 children. Whether this decrease in the rate of child abuse fatalities will continue cannot be determined at this point, but the rate will be monitored closely.

While most fatality data were obtained from State child welfare agencies, many of these agencies also received data from additional sources. For FFY 2005, nearly one-fifth (18.5%) of fatalities were reported through the Agency File, which includes fatalities reported by health departments and fatality review boards. The coordination of data collection with other agencies contributes to a fuller understanding of the size of the phenomenon, as well as to better estimation.

Age and sex of child fatalities. More than three-quarters (76.6%) of children who were killed were younger than 4 years of age, 13.4 percent were 4–7 years of age, 4.0 percent were 8–11 years of age, and 6.1 percent were 127–17 years of age.

Children whose families had received family preservation services in the past five years accounted for 11.7 percent of child fatalities.

The youngest children experienced the highest rates of fatalities. Infant boys (younger than 1 year) had a fatality rate of 17.3 deaths per 100,000 boys of the same age. Infant girls (younger than 1 year) had a fatality rate of 14.5 deaths per 100,000 girls of the same age. In general, fatality rates for both boys and girls decreased as the children get older.

Race and ethnicity of child fatalities. Nearly one-half (44.3 percent) of all fatalities were White children. One-quarter (26.0%) were African-American children, and nearly one-fifth (19.3 percent) were Hispanic children. Children of American Indian or Alaska Native, Asian, Pacific Islander, "other," and multiple race categories collectively accounted for 4.5 percent of fatalities.

Perpetrator relationships of child fatalities. Three-quarters (76.6%) of child fatalities were caused by one or more parent: More than one-quarter (28.5%) of fatalities were perpetrated by the mother acting alone. Nonparental perpetrators (e.g., other relative, foster parent, residential facility staff, "other," and legal guardian) were responsible for 13.0 percent of fatalities.

Maltreatment types of child fatalities. The three main categories of maltreatment related to fatalities were neglect (42.2%), combinations of maltreatments (27.3%), and physical abuse (24.1%). Medical neglect accounted for 2.5 percent of fatalities.

Prior CPS contact of child fatalities. Some children who died from maltreatment were already known to CPS agencies. Children whose families had received family preservation services in the past 5 years accounted for 11.7 percent of child fatalities. Nearly 3 percent (2.7%) of the child fatalities had been in foster care and were reunited with their families in the past 5 years. . . .

Perpetrators of Child Maltreatment

The National Child Abuse and Neglect Data System (NCANDS) defines a perpetrator as a person who is considered responsible for the maltreatment of a child. Thus, this [section] provides data about only those perpetrators of child abuse victims and does not include data about alleged perpetrators.

Given the definition of child abuse and neglect, which largely pertains to caregivers, most perpetrators of child maltreatment are parents. Other caregivers, including relatives, foster parents and residential facility staff also are included. During Federal fiscal year (FFY) 2005:

- Nearly 80 percent (79.4%) of perpetrators were parents of the victim;

- More than one-half (61.0%) of perpetrators neglected children; and

- Approximately 58 percent (57.8%) of perpetrators were women and 42.2 percent were men.

For the analyses in this [section], a perpetrator may be counted multiple times if he or she has maltreated more than one child. This presents data about the demographic characteristics of perpetrators, the relationship of perpetrators to their victims, and the types of maltreatment they committed.

Characteristics of Perpetrators

For FFY 2005, 57.8 percent of the perpetrators were women and 42.2 percent were men.

Women typically were younger than men. The median age of women was 31 years and 34 years for men. Of the women who were perpetrators, more than 40 percent (45.3%) were younger than 30 years of age, compared with one-third of the men (34.7%).

The racial distribution of perpetrators was similar to the race of their victims. During FFY 2005, more than one-half (55.1%) of perpetrators were White and one-fifth (20.9%) were African-American. Approximately 18 percent (17.6%) of perpetrators were Hispanic.

Nearly 80 percent (79.4%) of perpetrators were parents. Of the parents who were perpetrators, more than 90 percent (90.5%) were biological parents, 4.3 percent were stepparents, and 0.7 percent were adoptive parents. Other relatives accounted for an additional 6.8 percent. Unmarried partners of parents accounted for 3.8 percent.

More than one-half (61.0%) of all perpetrators were found to have neglected children. Slightly more than 10 percent (10.9%) of perpetrators physically abused children, and 7.7 percent sexually abused children. More than 10 percent (10.8%) of all perpetrators were associated with more than one type of maltreatment.

Intimate Partner Violence Affects Lesbian, Gay, Bisexual, and Transgender Relationships

Kim Fountain and Avy A. Skolnik

Kim Fountain is director of Community Organizing and Public Advocacy for the National Coalition of Anti-Violence Programs. Avy A. Skolnik is networks coordinator at the National Coalition of Anti-Violence Programs.

When someone is battered, they most often will benefit greatly from supportive and effective services. Unfortunately, for lesbian, gay, bisexual, and transgender (LGBT) IPV [intimate partner violence] survivors, such services are fraught with potentials for re-victimization that pivots on homophobia, transphobia, and heterosexism [the belief that heterosexuality is superior to other forms of sexual identification]. To this end, the deleterious effects of homophobia and heterosexism cannot be discounted in the lives of lesbian, gay, bisexual, and transgender (LGBT) survivors of IPV.

Survivors, regardless of their identities, often need help to negotiate the manipulation tactics and harm inflicted upon them by batterers. The types of harm they experience as well as the types of assistance they may need, however, are very much impacted by their perceived or actual identities. Batterers often use racism, homophobia, classism, ableism [discrimination based on disabilities], and any other tool of oppression to inflict harm. When such tactics are used, this compounds the effects of the violence and need for help. Support frequently comes from victim service providers in the form of shelter, safety planning, help with orders of protection, and court accompaniment. The aim for most providers is to make available the best possible services to victims in order to help them develop the safest possible options given the particular circumstances of the abuse and the relationship. Unfortunately, survivors from marginalized communities do not always receive services on par with those offered to mainstream survivors. As various cultures gain societal power and respect, they challenge inequities in myriad aspects of life, including IPV services.

Resisting Change

Not all providers, advocates, and victim services staff feel that they need to learn more about LGBT IPV. Several factors come into play informing this opinion. Many victim services staff are overworked and underpaid. Learning about expanding services to include culturally respectful and effective approaches to services is viewed across a wide range. People may be interested in learning something new, annoyed that they are being distracted from their "real" work, or angered by what they feel is liberal propaganda. There are also the attendant ways that the information that people learn is distilled and utilized.

For those who seek to institute changes they are often met with great resistance as such changes constitute a shift in the common understandings of domestic violence. In response to the difficulties of changing a system with few resources, providers often fall back upon a "one size fits all" mode of thinking. They may feel that by treating all DV [domestic violence] survivors "equally" they are doing the right thing. This is analogous to claims of "color blind" services where people claim to not see the color of another's skin when making decisions. While ideal in theory, in practice, it is dangerous.

As sociologist Margaret L. Andersen points out, "Public beliefs about race and gender are framed by implicit liberal philosophy, presuming color-and gender-blindness as the ideal. But this masks the continuing inequities involving race, class, and gender."

Such claims to serve all equally without regard to sexuality, while sincere, miss the point that intimate partner violence occurs in a homophobic and heterosexist culture that works to limit the lives of LGBT people. Ignoring this is almost certain to cause further harm to LGBT survivors and does little to challenge the oppression. This report helps to demonstrate the extent to which IPV exists in the LGBT communities as well as some of the points of re-victimization that are enacted when services are sought.

"Internalized Homophobia"

For many LGBT survivors of IPV, the harm enacted against them occurs at the confluence of streams of violence in the forms of bias and hatred that spring forth from interpersonal, institutional, and cultural points of origin. Experiencing victimization through societal stigma leaves many LGBT people vulnerable to commonly used tools of manipulation of batterers. Quite often, early experiences of bias and hatred results in a form of victimization that erodes the self-worth of the survivor based upon self-hatred. This is commonly known as internalized homophobia.

As with many other forms of victimization that carry societal stigma and whose victims are often silenced, such as sexual assault and trafficking, it is estimated that those who do not come forward far outnumber those who do come forward.

Service providers and their agencies do not always recognize how LGBT-related bias impacts survivors. Much of this is due to the fact that traditional domestic violence models are based upon heteronormative conceptions of power dynamics and relationships and they do not tend to take into account the experiences of social stigma in the lifespan of an individual. Together, these two tendencies in service provision make accessing and utilizing IPV services more of an obstacle than a help for many LGBT IPV survivors.

Through a strong legacy provided by the domestic violence movement over the past thirty years, it is clear that to address, and eventually stop batterers, change needs to occur at societal levels through legislation, training, education, and the production of viable and effective options for survivors. Unfortunately, because the mainstream domestic violence movement relies heavily upon hetero-normative (and thus) homophobic practices, LGBT survivors, if they make it past internalized homophobia to accessing services, often suffer re-victimization. NCAVP [National Coalition of Anti-Violence Program] exists, in part, to both remedy these inequalities and to offer services to LGBT IPV survivors . . . , advocating with other providers and law enforcement for equal services, ensuring equitable representation in legislative proposals, and to educating the LGBT public around issues of IPV.

It is important that providers and other victim services personnel have an understanding of the intertwined experiences of bias and intimate partner violence.

As with many other forms of victimization that carry societal stigma and whose victims are often silenced, such as sexual assault and trafficking, it is estimated that those who do not come forward far outnumber those who do come forward. The statistics recorded . . . therefore, should be taken to represent only a fraction of the LGBT intimate partner violence that occurs throughout the United States every year. As service providers and community members we speak with people living in DV situations every day, and know that many more continue to suffer silently or unheard within abusive relationships. To help ensure that one day, all IPV survivors will be able to make decisions from a full set of service options, NCAVP and contributors to this report have made a commitment to documenting and reporting the cases of IPV we see each year.

In a highly charged political arena in which many LGBT groups, agencies, and organizations use the "but we are just like everyone else" argument in order to gain equality in everything from marriage to access to orders of protection, NCAVP is a daily witness to the ways in which while LGBT people indeed do reflect the incredible diversity within the United States, we are also different from other groups in ways that may leave us open to homophobia and heterosexism. It is the use, unintentional and otherwise, of these societal tools of oppression within the arena of IPV that are addressed in the next section.

Anti-LGBT Violence

LGBT bias strongly affects the experiences of LGBT people across a lifespan. The emphasis on lifespan is crucial because it helps to situate how many victims may frame the intimate partner violence in their lives. Such framing will greatly influence the ways that services are sought, engaged, and utilized. To this end, it is important that providers and other victim services personnel have an understanding of the intertwined experiences of bias and intimate partner violence. . . .

Many of the survival skills learned in surviving abuse in youth extend to relationship building in later life:

- If one can hide their sexuality, chances are rather good that the person can hide IPV. Both are highly stigmatized.

- Further, it is that much more difficult to access services if one does not have the language for what is happening because the main messages involve negative stereotyping.

49

- If one is not out, it may be stressful to try to find services.

- Isolation is one of the strongest weapons that a batterer uses. If one is already many times removed from support because people have abandoned them, then a batterer's work is that much easier. Many youth do not have an opportunity to build a large LGBT community unless they belong to groups, which means being able to get to the group as well as being able to tell your parent or guardian where you are going, or lying.

Surviving into adulthood is a challenge for youth who have been taught that part of their identity is sick, sinful, a mistake, unnatural, etc., that they should hide who they are, that adults who are supposed to provide safety and care cannot be trusted, and that the systems that they are expected to support are not designed to help them. These youth also often prove to be incredibly resilient. Unfortunately, as with heterosexual adults, many become involved with batterers who rely upon societal tools of oppression and who count on homophobic or heterosexist systems and providers to allow the battering to continue.

It is important to note that all barriers present in both prevention and intervention of LGBT intimate partner violence are rooted in sexism, heterosexism, and transphobia.

The Impact of Homophobia and Transphobia on Domestic Violence

Tools that may be used by the batterer to gain and maintain control are often highly individualized to the situation, relationship and people involved. It is important in any given situation of IPV to investigate the way the survivor defines the abuse and understand the ways that behaviors which we may not traditionally see as typically abusive can be utilized as such in a context where IPV already exists. However, there are several tactics that are commonly used by batterers against their victims. These behaviors may include:

- Verbal abuse such as name calling

- Emotional manipulation

- Isolation, including limiting or prohibiting a partner's contact with family or friends

- Stealing, limiting access to or destroying a partner's property

- Withholding or otherwise controlling or restricting access to finances

- Depriving partner of shelter, food, clothing, sleep, medication or any other life-sustaining mechanism

- Limiting or prohibiting a partner from obtaining or keeping employment, housing or any other station, benefit or service

- Harming or attempting to harm a partner physically

- Harming or threatening harm to partner's family, friends, children and/or pets

- Sexually assaulting or raping a partner

- Using intentional exposure to sexually-transmitted and other diseases

- Threatening suicide or harm to self, if a partner tries to end a relationship or does not comply with an abuser's demands

- Stalking or harassing a partner

- Using facets of abuser or survivor's identity including race, gender, class, sexual orientation, national origin, physical ability, religion, level of education, occupation, or legal immigration status, etc., to demean, insult, endanger, isolate, or otherwise oppress

All of the above tactics may be used by a batterer. There are additional concerns for LGBT survivors. LGBT domestic violence is as prevalent as heterosexual domestic violence. And perpetrators often attempt highly specific forms of abuse including:

- "Outing" or threatening to out a partner's sexual orientation or gender identity to family, employer, police, religious institution, community, or in child custody disputes

- Reinforcing fears that no one will help a partner because s/he is lesbian, gay, bisexual or transgender, or that for this reason, the partner "deserves" the abuse

- Alternatively, justifying abuse with the notion that a partner is not "really" lesbian, gay, bisexual or transgender; i.e., s/he may once have had or may still have relationships with other people, or express a gender identity, inconsistent with the abuser's definitions of these terms

- Telling the partner that abusive behavior is a normal part of LGBT relationships, or that it cannot be domestic violence because it is occurring between LGBT individuals

Following the work of Kimberle Crenshaw on intersectionality, defined as "The need to account for multiple grounds of identity when considering how the social world is constructed," NCAVP recognizes that no one experiences life or moments of oppression through a singular understanding of his or her identity. For instance, when an African American lesbian is attacked on the street, she experiences the attack as an African American person, a lesbian, a woman, and any number of other identities, and in the context of all her past experiences of violence and bias. This report, while focusing on LGBT identities, recognizes that there is no monolithic LGBT identity and that there is a significant need to work with people as full individuals.

It is important to note that all barriers present in both prevention and intervention of LGBT intimate partner violence are rooted in sexism, heterosexism, and transphobia. These attitudes, though often unspoken, are still pervasive in our police departments, court systems, medical centers, shelters, and organizations. The butch lesbian survivor in shelter who is watched more closely by staff than her fellow more feminine heterosexual fellow residents; the gay man who stays at all-night diners and couch hops with friends because he cannot access DV shelter or homeless shelter; the transwoman who is arrested and placed in a men's jail cell along with her abusive boyfriend because the officer "believes" she provoked a fight; the transman who is denied an order of protection in court because the judge refuses to acknowledge that his girlfriend is a real threat to his safety. Policy and legislation change alone will not eliminate these barriers for our communities.

"Outing" LGBT Intimate Partner Violence

Over the past several years, many articles, websites, and a handful of books have been written to address LGBT battering. Some take a statistical approach in order to "prove" that [LGBT] IPV exists, others move toward more anecdotal stories to let victims and survivors speak of their own experiences, and others rely upon a legal or ethnographic/historic approach. Combined, these essays, articles and books represent a genealogy that begins to substantively take shape with the second wave of feminism and proceeds forward through queer theory. As these sources, combined with past NCAVP reports, indicate, LGBT IPV does exist.

Intimate Partner Violence services that rely solely or predominantly on the rule that "men beat women while they are in relationships" miss the centrality of the workings of power and control in domestic violence. Rather than focusing on the dynamics of power and control, they focus upon the gender relationships and the assumed roles within the relationships. This method misses the thousands of victims that do not fit this model. It also misses the nuances of how power and oppression affect each of us individually, from the moment we are born. For a survivor who accesses services, their identities will also impact many aspects of these experiences. Differences between the material and symbolic experiences of LGBT victims and those of heterosexual victims are held in tension through the heteronormative imperative within the prevailing discourse on IPV that frames LGBT victims ultimately as less than or an additional burden. Difference becomes the focus of exclusion and reinforcement of normal behavior rather than an opportunity to expand the scope of services. Far too little is done to compensate for the discrepancies in services, leaving already vulnerable populations subject to further harm. An enormous shift must occur that allows providers to identify how power and oppression work in the lives of individuals with intersecting identities.

Publicly exposing the effects of heterosexism, homophobia, and transphobia within IPV and within our institutions helps combat the stigma inflicted upon LGBT people by breaking the conspiracy of silence that society demands of them. As LGBT people work to lift the stigma that keeps many people in some way shamed or silenced about their experiences of abuse, or wary of sharing their identity, we begin to move closer to a day when LGBT victims and survivors are adequately and fairly provided services, including orders of protection, real safety planning, and shelter. And closer to a day when no single person experiences violence from those they love.

Siblings, Parents, and Pets Can Be Victims of Family Violence

Karel Kurst-Swanger and Jacqueline L. Petcosky

Karel Kurst-Swanger is an assistant professor of public justice in the Department of Public Justice at the State University of New York-Oswego. Jacqueline L. Petcosky is a customer service advocate for New York State Electric and Gas.

As is true for all forms of violence in the home . . . , there is no one clear explanation for the occurrence of sibling abuse. . . . Understanding why violence occurs between siblings requires an examination of the individual, the family system, and the social conditions present within a given society. Because the varying forms of sibling abuse occur so frequently, we should explore some of the factors that we know or suspect are associated specifically with abusive behaviors between siblings.

Factors Associated with Sibling Abuse

Issues of power and control. [I]ssues of power and control weigh heavily in abusive relationships. When power differentials exist, the potential for abuse exists. In the case of siblings, power may be determined by birth order, gender, or size. Therefore, siblings who have more "natural power" are in a position to victimize children in the family who have less.

However, when it comes to children, another factor is also important to consider. How power is distributed or utilized by siblings may be determined by parental behavior. For example, an older sister may be left with the responsibility of caring for a younger sister. The authority granted to the older sister through the designation of the title "baby-sitter" may create a potential situation in which abuse can occur. [V.R.] Wiehe notes that parents often have unrealistic expectations of their older children's ability to responsibly care for younger siblings, creating a circumstance in which normal conflicts can be played out in an abusive way. Some siblings are simply too young to be left in charge, and others, although arguably old enough, lack the appropriate "parenting" skills to adequately perform the necessary functions of baby-sitters.

Lack of supervision and nonintervention. Although all siblings, with the possible exception of some twin pairs, have some level of power inequality in that one of them has to be older, bigger, and so forth, power inequities combined with parental behavior may be the determining factors in how sibling interactions will ultimately be played out. The lack of appropriate adult supervision, or the lack of parental intervention, provides an opportunity for abusive acts to occur. For example, siblings who engage in more predatory behavior, such as sexual abuse, generally require adult absences in order to be successful in their attempts to victimize. When adults are not supervising sibling interactions, the inequitable distribution of power is more likely to be an issue in sibling relationships.

Additionally, parents who do not intervene in sibling acts of abuse when they witness or are told of such events are, in effect, reinforcing the inequitable distribution of power and the inappropriate behavior. For example, a study conducted by [L.] Kramer, [L.A.] Perozynski, and [T.] Chung found that parental nonintervention in the sibling conflicts between their children (who had a 2- to 4-year age differential) was highly associated with the continued occurrence of additional events. In their study of 88 two-child, two-parent families, they found that younger children, in particular, were far more combative when their parents did not intervene. . . .

Family dysfunction. The research we have discussed in this [essay] points to overall family dysfunction, family stress, and intrafamilial abuse as being common themes present in families with siblings who are abusive. These research findings are consistent with two main theoretical perspectives, attachment theory and social learning theory. In other words, how we interact with others is a result of our early experiences with human interaction.

Problems such as drug and alcohol abuse, mental illness, marital discord, and financial stresses can overload parents, rendering them ineffective in areas of discipline and supervision.

Specifically, attachment theory examines sibling relationships as a result of the internalization of interactions with a child's primary caregivers. Social learning theory suggests that abusive behavior by parents is reinforced over time and eventually is generalized to sibling, and perhaps even peer, relationships. In either theoretical perspective, a child's social behavior is related to the interactional patterns within the family. Therefore, such interactions as resolving conflicts, showing affection, discipline, sexual behavior, power distribution, and so forth are exhibited, reinforced, and internalized by children as they grow. Children then take what they have learned and apply it to other situations. There may even be an additive quality to such behaviors. For example, [a 2000 study] found that young boys who experienced high levels of destructive sibling conflict and high levels of parental rejection were more likely to exhibit aggressive behaviors, both at home and at school, than children who experienced only one of these predictors.

Therefore, families teach children about social behavior through modeling and reinforcement. Families who exhibit violent, abusive behavior are likely to find siblings reacting in similar ways. Social behavior is learned from a variety of influences; however, parents' interactions with each other and with their children do provide young children with a foundation on which to build their repertoire of behaviors. Therefore, it is not surprising that research continues to find linkages between child maltreatment, intimate partner abuse, and child-perpetrated violence.

Another factor in sibling abuse may be the inability of the parent to provide adequate parenting due to some other level of dysfunction. Wiehe notes that sibling abuse often occurs in families in which the parents are overwhelmed with their own problems and therefore are unable or unwilling to intervene in the problems of their children. Problems such as drug and alcohol abuse, mental illness, marital discord, and financial stresses can overload parents, rendering them ineffective in areas of discipline and supervision.

Social conditions. We must also include the role of various social conditions in the perpetuation of sibling abuse. First, given the general acceptance of acts of sibling abuse in the larger social structure, even young people who live in relatively healthy families can experience sibling abuse. As we discussed earlier, current social standards regard physical acts of aggression between siblings as normal sibling rivalry. Therefore, parents may receive little guidance from their social support network of family and friends to assist them in appropriate levels of intervention into destructive sibling interactions. Communities dismiss sibling violence as a natural occurrence that children ultimately grow out of; therefore, it is not considered serious. The lack of concern over sibling abuse is evident in the lack of public policy and social service response systems to intervene in such situations. However, although sibling violence does tend to dissipate over time, [Megan P.] Goodwin and [Bruce] Roscoe point out that, when older youths are still engaged in destructive behaviors, there is a greater risk of serious injury due to their size and physical strength. Additionally, we cannot dismiss the consequence that behavior learned and reinforced in childhood is often continued into later adulthood.

Second, economic forces often create circumstances in which families become vulnerable to abusive behavior by siblings. For example, if both parents must work or choose to work outside the home, children may be left alone to care for themselves. Families may lack appropriate financial resources to provide adequate child care, housing arrangements in which siblings have a level of privacy, and the ability to access appropriate services for themselves or their children.

Consequences of Sibling Abuse

As with all other forms of violence in the home, sibling abuse has devastating consequences for the victim and the family. Recently, research has begun to explore the ways in which sibling relationships influence development, psychological functioning, and social behavior. However, only a handful of studies have focused on the effects of sibling abuse in particular.

In his study of survivors of sibling abuse, Wiehe found that victims suffered from many long-term problems as a result of acts of abuse by their siblings. Perhaps the most pervasive finding was the impact on the victim's self-esteem. Self-esteem is frequently affected by abuse. Victims are left feeling insignificant, degraded, worthless, and unloved. Additionally, survivors reported having difficulty with relationships with the opposite sex and others; repeating the victim role in other relationships; self-blame, anger, and resentment toward the perpetrator; sexual dysfunction; eating disorders; alcoholism and drug abuse; depression; and posttraumatic stress disorder.

[E.] Garrett and [B.] McKenzie found that victims of sibling abuse suffer the same type of long-term effects as do victims of other kinds of child maltreatment. Consequences included difficulties with other interpersonal relationships and sexual functioning and emotional problems. Victims also reported low self-esteem as a direct result of being insulted by a sibling regarding their appearance, height, weight, and personality. Additionally, [Sandra A.] Graham-Bermann and associates found that the emotional toll of sibling violence was greater for females than for males and was associated with feelings of anxiety in young adulthood.

Parents may actually go to great lengths to protect their abusive children and keep up the appearance of a happy family life.

These studies provide evidence that sibling abuse is a serious phenomenon with consequences as devastating as those of other forms of violence in the home. However, the public discussion of sibling abuse has not yet been realized as fully as it has for other forms of family violence. Therefore, little aid is currently available in terms of prevention and intervention. Child welfare workers are bound by state policies that examine only the abusive acts of adults in the home. Therefore, parents would have to step forward to report their children to the police or juvenile court to seek intervention. Given the general lack of public recognition of sibling abuse issues, it is unlikely that parents would seek the assistance of the police and courts in such circumstances unless the violence resulted in serious physical injury or was one among other inappropriate behaviors, such as running away, truancy, fighting with peers, substance abuse, or acts of delinquency.

Parental Abuse

Many of us can recall having fights or disagreements with our parents during our growing years. In fact, many us may even consider conflict with parents a normal "rite of passage" from adolescence into adulthood. However, the idea of a young person physically attacking or threatening violence against a parent seems incomprehensible. As parents have more control and power by virtue of their age, size, and access to financial resources, how can they possibly be victims of family violence? However difficult this may be for us to imagine, the truth is that some children do abuse their parents. . . . In this section we restrict our discussion to children and adolescents who abuse their parents.

Although the research and experiences of juvenile justice professionals clearly documents the existence of parental abuse, measuring actual prevalence rates has been difficult. As you might imagine, parents do not often report such incidents to authorities due to embarrassment and fear of getting the child into trouble or of the child retaliating. Parents may actually go to great lengths to protect abusive children and keep up the appearance of a happy family life. [Richard J.] Gelles describes the social disapproval of children using force against a parent as being a factor in parents' reasons for not routinely disclosing such behavior.

Children who are violent toward a parent often have had a past history of victimization by a parent, either directly or through the observation of intimate partner violence.

Although parents may not openly discuss such behavior, often young people who are abusive to their parents also exhibit other behavioral problems, such as running away from home, difficulties at school, alcohol and drug use, delinquency, and so forth, and thereby come to the attention of the juvenile justice system. Thus probation officers, family court personnel, and social service workers routinely come across youths who are abusive to one or both parents.

Outside the experience of juvenile justice professionals, the measurement of violence against parents has not drawn the attention of researchers in a broad way, as other forms of family violence have. [Claire P.] Cornell and Gelles found that in a nationally representative sample of families who had a teenager living at home, 9 percent of the parents reported that at least one act of violence had been perpetrated by their child against them. Gelles argues that although this 9 percent may sound like an insignificant percentage, it translates into 2.5 million parents who are assaulted at least once a year by one of their children. Additionally, [C.] Peek, [J.L.] Fisher, and [J.S.] Kidwell estimated that 8 percent of fathers and 6 percent of mothers have been victimized by their children. More recently, [Kevin D.] Browne and [Catherine E.] Hamilton found similar results, with 8.5 percent of mothers and 6.1 percent of fathers experiencing violence by a child. According to the National Crime Victimization Survey, of the more than 7 million crimes of violence reported by victims, 68,150 were perpetrated by a child against a parent.

Why are children abusive toward their parents? The answer seems to lie in the complexity of violent families themselves. Children who are violent toward a parent often have had a past history of victimization by a parent, either directly or through the observation of intimate partner violence. Being part of a violent family teaches young people to use violence to mediate their conflicts, and observing such violence consequently leads to child behavioral problems. We also know that adolescents who have friends who assault their parents, who find some delinquent behaviors reasonable, who perceive the risk of getting caught to be very low, or who have weak attachments to their parents are also at risk for being abusive to a parent.

Our understanding of other forms of violence between child and parent is even more unclear. To date, little is known about possible emotional or sexual abuse by children against a parent. Most of the research has focused on physical assault. However, children killing parents has gained more attention from researchers.

Parricide

Parricide refers to killing one's own parent. *Patricide* is the murder of one's father, and *matricide* is the murder of one's mother.

Parricide has recently come to the public's attention because of the highly publicized case of the Menendez brothers in 1989. In this case, Erik and Lyle Menendez were found guilty of murdering their wealthy socialite parents in Los Angeles. The defense argued that Erik and Lyle had suffered past physical abuse by their father and believed that they were in danger of death or imminent serious bodily harm. The prosecution, however, argued that Erik and Lyle killed their parents to gain control of their parent's wealth. The first trial ended with a deadlocked jury, but the second trial jury was not convinced of their reports of past abuse. In 1996, the jury found the brothers guilty of first-degree murder with a special circumstance of financial gain, which carried a mandatory life-without-parole sentence. Although the brothers have appealed the convictions, the state Supreme Court ruled to uphold their convictions.

Some 300 parents and stepparents are murdered each year in the United States by their children or stepchildren. Approximately 1.5 to 2.5 percent of all homicides in the United States are parricides. Both adults and youths, particularly those in late adolescence, have been responsible for the death of parents. . . .

Victims of parricide are typically white and non-Hispanic and are in their late 40s or 50s. Perpetrators tend to be white, non-Hispanic males, and more than 70 percent of them are younger than 30 years old. Although we have been unable to determine the exact number of homicides involving young offspring because of limitations in data collection, [K.] Heide estimates that as many as 65 natural parents (45 fathers and 20 mothers) have been killed by children under the age of 18.

In a review of the literature on adolescent parricide, Heide notes that the majority of studies conducted on the subject have found widespread evidence of child maltreatment and spousal abuse. Therefore, other forms of violence in the home are important to our understanding of the reasons that a

young person would kill one or both of his or her parents. . . .
Child victims of abuse and neglect often suffer many consequences, including later violent behavior. In a study involving
40 women who were abused as children, Heide and [E.P.] So-
lomon discovered that half of them had seriously considered
killing their parents to escape ongoing sexual abuse. Many of
the women reported that they did not ultimately murder their
parents for fear that they lacked the speed, agility, or strength
necessary to complete the act.

In addition to finding evidence of family violence, Heide
has identified several other characteristics that tend to be associated with adolescent parricide. These include easy access
to guns, failed efforts by the adolescent to secure help or escape from the family situation, social isolation, alcohol abuse
in the home, and increased feelings of helplessness and an inability to cope with stress. Also this crime often involves youths
who have not had any prior involvement in the justice system.
Heide also found evidence that family members have felt relieved by the death of the parent. This finding relates to the
work of [D.] Sargent and [C.P.] Ewing, who have observed
that in some cases of parricide a conspiracy exists in which
the adolescent more or less acts on behalf of the rest of the
family by killing the parent. The adolescent responds to direct
or indirect messages from other family members who wish
the parent dead.

Fewer cases of adolescent parricide can be attributed to
mental illness. Sometimes the parricide is preceded by a long
history of psychiatric problems, and in some cases the parricide event becomes the first obvious sign of illness. However,
especially in the case of adolescents, often the perpetrator suf-
fers from acute depression and suicidal ideation.

Even fewer cases have been identified in which the motive
for killing is greed. Even when economic gain can clearly be
established, often it is also associated with long-term child
maltreatment, antisocial behavior, or both. . . .

Defining Animal Abuse

All kinds of animals have been subjected to cruelty by family members. Actual violence, threats of violence, and neglect have been perpetrated on family pets such as birds, cats, dogs, fish, and turtles, on livestock such as goats, pigs, sheep, turkeys, rabbits, and horses, and on wild or stray animals. However, the task of identifying animal abuse in the context of family violence requires a clear definition of *animal* and of what constitutes *abusive treatment*. The legal definitions present in animal welfare legislation often have specific language defining what an animal is or is not. For example, Delaware defines animals as "excluding fish, crustaceans, and mollusks," Kentucky refers to "four-legged animals." Additionally, the criteria used to determine what types of behavior are to be considered maltreatment must also be well established within statutes. Behaviors such as hunting, mercy killing, killing animals for food, using force or prodding instruments for training purposes, using animals in entertainment, and so forth are socially accepted practices. The motivation for animal mistreatment is an important feature of the family violence dynamic. The reasons behind such cruelty to animals, especially by children, are complex and varied.

When the intention to harm animals is purely a result of the dynamics of abusive family relationships, the context and definition of animal maltreatment should be explored further by legislators, veterinarians, animal welfare workers, criminal justice professionals, clinicians, victim advocates, and researchers. One of the first attempts to begin to categorize animal violence has recently been developed by Barbara Boat. The Boat Inventory on Animal-Related Experiences (BIARE) was developed to gain assessment information from children and adults about the role of animal-focused violence in their histories. The inventory examines the history of pet ownership, experiences of animals as a source of support, experiences of participating in or witnessing acts of cruelty, killing, or sexual interactions, and animal fears. Although the inventory has been utilized or adapted for use in only a handful of studies, it provides the initial dialogue on animal abuse in the lives of individuals in need of mental health services.

Following are a variety of examples of the numerous ways in which animals have been abused by family members. However, standards for what kinds of circumstances actually constitute cruelty vary widely in state laws and local ordinances.

Physical abuse. Like humans, animals have suffered injuries from being hit, kicked, thrown across the room, stabbed or cut, jumped on, lit on fire, blinded, stoned, trapped, strangled, and so forth. Physical abuse may involve acts meant to torture animals (and their human victims) or to tease them; however, the intention is to cause suffering and pain.

Neglect. The vast majority of acts of cruelty to animals involve neglect.... Neglect generally refers to a lack of proper provision of food, shelter, and reasonable medical treatment and the failure to euthanize an animal when medically indicated. However, the standards of care for various types of animals are not well established, making the diagnosis of neglect very difficult. Emotional neglect is one area in which such standards are not clear. For example, many would agree that keeping dogs isolated for long periods of time has a negative impact on dogs; however, statutes may not address inhumane restraint. Neglect may be a deliberate act of an abuser to gain control over a victim or a passive act as part of an overall picture of neglect for family members.

Sexual abuse. Animals are also sexually abused in numerous ways. Adults or children may be forced into acts of or witnessing bestiality by their abusive partners or parents. Abuse might include sexual touching of animals, inserting objects into an animal's orifices, sodomy, and actual intercourse.

Peticide. Peticide can be defined as the willful, deliberate, unjustified slaying of a companion animal, with the specific intent to intimidate, terrorize, or emotionally blackmail the animal's owner. Death is often of the most violent nature, including mutilation, being set on fire, decapitation, hanging, shooting, placing an animal in a microwave oven, tying an animal to railroad tracks, leaving an injured animal in the road, and so forth.

Signs of abuse. Regardless of the form abuse takes, both animals and humans are profoundly affected by such maltreatment. Sherry Schlueter outlines standard signs of abuse, which include:

- Animals in poor physical condition.

- Animals that are excessively aggressive or submissive.

- Poor general sanitation of animal living area.

- Space, light, and ventilation deficiencies.

- Excessive numbers of animals for the space and other resources.

- Cruel confinement.

- Lack of necessary medical care or absence of appropriate food.

- Evidence of dead animals, buried or unburied, on the property.

- Having species in locations where they are not permitted by zoning regulations.

- Financial inability to properly feed or care for animals.

- Evidence of bestiality.

- Evidence of ritualistic sacrifice.

- Evidence of animal baiting and fighting.

- Humans and pets living in a state of isolation.

- Excessive matting of hair coat.

- Parasite infestation.

- Abandonment of animals. . . .

Link Between Animal Abuse and Intimate Partner Abuse

Stories of women who have been abused by their intimate partners are often filled with examples of brutality toward pets. Although ample anecdotal information is available from domestic violence advocates and treatment professionals, little has been done to formally document the extent of animal abuse in violent homes. It is theorized that abusers use violence toward pets as a way of demanding control and further threatening intimate partners, and this violence may in fact be related to the batterer's lethality.

In an effort to begin to document such abuses, the Center for Prevention of Domestic Violence developed a protocol to identify and categorize violence toward animals in three programs that serve both victims and batterers. During the years 1993 through 1996, these programs asked victims and offenders questions regarding animals being threatened, abused, and killed. Interestingly, 12 percent of the victims who were served in the advocacy program during this time period reported that their partners had threatened, abused, or killed a family pet, and 15.5 percent of the women residing in the safe house reported such abuses. However, only .09 percent of the batterers completing the MOVE (Men Overcoming Violent Encounters) program took responsibility for such acts. The center documented both direct and indirect forms of abuse toward animals. Examples of direct forms of abuse included kicking the dog or cat; throwing an animal across the room, shooting the animal (often in front of the victim), breaking the pet's legs or neck, hanging the pet, cutting ears or tails, and so forth. Indirect forms of abuse included abandoning the pet; neglecting to feed or water farm animals, threatening to take the pet away, euthanizing pets to retaliate against human victims, threatening to kill and cook the pet rabbit, overfeeding fish, and making an asthmatic woman live in a house with long-haired cats.

In a study of battered women who were residing at a shelter in northern Utah, Frank Ascione found that of the women who owned pets, 71 percent reported that their male partners had threatened, hurt, or killed one or more of their pets. Women reported examples such as threatening to put a kitten in a blender, burying a cat up to its head and mowing it, and starving a dog. Animals were slapped, shaken, thrown, drowned, lit on fire, and shot by their abusive partners. Additionally, 18 percent of the women noted that they did not seek help earlier for fear of what would happen to their pets if they left.

In a national survey of domestic violence shelters, [Frank R.] Ascione, [C.V.] Weber, and [D.S.] Wood investigated shelter professionals' perceptions of the connection between battering and animal abuse. They found that, although the majority of shelters reported that their adult and child clients talked about incidents of pet abuse, few shelters routinely inquired about animal abuse in their intake interview processes. In addition, only 8 percent of the respondents reported collaborative arrangements with animal welfare professionals to provide shelter for pets.

Link Between Animal Abuse and Child Maltreatment

Examining the link between child abuse and animal abuse has also generated substantial evidence worthy of further investigation. Research has focused on the clinical connection between children who are cruel to animals and past victimization. Children who have witnessed domestic violence or have suffered directly through the hands of an abusive parent may respond by being cruel to animals. [E.] DeViney, [J.] Dickert, and [R.] Lockwood were the first to explore the relationship between child maltreatment and the abuse of pets. In this early study [1983] of 53 New Jersey families indicated for child abuse, 88 percent of the families who physically abused their children also had animals that were abused, as compared with only 34 percent of the families who abused their children in a different manner. In this study, both fathers and children were the perpetrators of animal-focused violence.

DeViney and colleagues suggested that children engaged in cruel behaviors toward animals as a way to scapegoat their problems toward a more powerless creature. Although this makes intuitive sense, the link between animal abuse and family violence may also suggest that children engage in aggressive acts toward animals as a way of modeling the behavior of an abusive parent or because of psychopathology. Understanding the complex dynamic of cruelty to animals by children is of serious concern, especially to mental health specialists. In fact, the American Psychiatric Association's *Diagnostic and Statistical Manual of Mental Disorders* (DSM-III-R) added physical cruelty to animals to the list of criteria to meet the diagnosis of conduct disorder. Conduct disorder is defined as "a persistent pattern of conduct in which the basic rights of others and major age-appropriate societal norms or rules are violated" (as cited in [P.] Arkow).

Clinical studies of violent adults and youths have acknowledged an association between childhood violence toward animals and later violence toward humans. Although the research has been limited, there appears to be a strong link between the experience of harsh physical punishment and to the commission of animal abuse in childhood, especially for males. Aggressive acts toward animals by children serves as an important indicator of future mental health problems and human violence. [C.P.] Flynn found a relationship between parent-to-child violence and animal abuse. He examined the connection between socially sanctioned corporal punishment and animal abuse. He found specifically that male-to-male violence (in the form of corporal punishment) had the strongest relationship to animal abuse, even among a nonclinical sample of college students. Aggression and dominance by males (exhibited by parents through corporal punishment) may be rehearsed by young males through aggressive acts toward animals.

Future Prevention and Intervention

Regardless of the forms that violence and aggression take in the home, animals are likely to be at risk for injury and suffering. In fact, Arkow states, "It is rare to see cases of severe animal abuse and neglect in which other problems are not also extant." Therefore, it is imperative that child welfare workers, family violence specialists, criminal justice professionals, mental health providers, and animal welfare professionals join together to protect animals within the context of violent families. Animal abuse serves as a marker for family violence, and in the same vein, family violence serves as a marker for animal abuse. The mutual goals of human welfare workers and animal welfare professionals demand a collaborative approach.

Additionally, although there is arguably ample legislation to protect animals, veterinarians have been reluctant to report cases of animal mistreatment, let alone suspected cases of family violence. To date, no legislation exists that requires veterinarians to report such maltreatment, although the ethical guidelines set forth by the profession do direct veterinarians to do so. Family violence specialists have not acknowledged the connection between animals and people and rarely consider family animals in traditional intervention systems. The bottom line is that animal abuse is a warning sign, one that begs our attention, not only for the future protection of animals but also for the future protection of humans.

CHAPTER 2

What Contributes to Family Violence?

Chapter Preface

Family violence is cyclical; its causes and effects often are the very same factors, and it can be difficult to determine the precise triggers of violence. As the adage goes, violence begets violence. In the case of family violence, one generation after another may be trapped in the pattern, with no understanding of when it began or how to make it stop. Poverty, emotional disturbances, unequal gender roles, substance abuse, and a stressful home environment all have the potential to lead an unstable person to outbursts of violence against family members. And such outbursts tend to lead to self-perpetuating problems that cause more of the same behavior and exacerbate other problems. For example, poverty or stress can cause an alcoholic to drink more, making him less emotionally stable and more likely to try to dominate his partner. In turn, he may lose his job due to his drinking, fall deeper into financial distress, and lash out even more.

Studies have shown that the long-term effects of family violence can be nearly as bad as the immediate results of battering. The worst-case scenario, of course, is the death of the victim. But repeatedly witnessing the abuse of a parent has the potential to cause numerous physical and emotional problems in children, from insomnia, headaches, and stomach pain to later abusive behavior in their own intimate relationships. According to a 2006 study by Gregory K. Moffatt, children, even babies, in homes where domestic violence occurs are victims even if they are not physically abused themselves:

> Not only are these children at risk for physical neglect and injury, but they are also at risk for both short-term problems such as post-traumatic stress disorder as well as long-term issues such as behavioral problems, mental health problems, sleep difficulties, and school problems. Even infants who are incapable of social awareness of the violence occur-

ring in their presence suffer long-term effects. In fact, research indicates that infants and toddlers through age three may be at higher risk for permanent damage than older children due to the plasticity of their developing brains. Measurable structural differences exist in the brains of children who have witnessed conjugal violence as infants and toddlers and these changes may be the source of a host of adolescent and adult psychiatric disorders.

Because its reach is so extensive and so damaging, physicians have begun to think of family violence as a public health issue. One study, published in the *International Journal of Epidemiology* in June 2007, indicates that children who live with family violence are at a higher risk of developing asthma. For African American women, intimate partner violence is one of the leading causes of death and disabling injuries. In 2003 the Centers for Disease Control and Prevention estimated that intimate partner violence against American women over the age of eighteen costs nearly $6 billion per year, $4.1 billion of which is for immediate medical and mental health care and $0.9 billion each for lost productivity at work and lifetime lost income from domestic violence-related homicides. These estimates do not include the costs of family violence against men, children, the elderly, the disabled, and income-providing animals such as livestock.

The selections in this chapter describe the factors that most often contribute to incidents of family violence. Rarely, however, is one contributing factor alone enough to create violence in families. Rather, as the authors discuss, several contributing factors coincide to create the problem, with each factor playing a role in the overall cycle.

Poverty, Power Imbalances, and Male Identity Contribute to Family Violence

Rachel Jewkes

Rachel Jewkes is the director of the Gender and Health Unit of South Africa's Medical Research Council. Trained as a medical doctor, she specializes in public health medicine.

With the exception of poverty, most demographic and social characteristics of men and women documented in survey research are not associated with increased risk of intimate partner violence. Age, for example, has occasionally been noted to be a risk factor for such violence, with a greater risk attached to youth, but in most research a relation with age of either partner has not been seen. Similarly, age at marriage is not an associated factor.

Intimate partner violence is mainly a feature of sexual relationships or thwarted sexual relationships in the case of stalking violence. Its relation with marital status varies between settings and is at least partly dependent on the extent to which women have premarital and extramarital sexual relationships. In countries such as Nicaragua where such sexual relationships are rare, intimate partner violence is closely linked to marriage. Where premarital sex is the norm, marital status is not associated with violence. In North America there is a high prevalence of violent experiences in separated or divorced women, but this has not been noted in other countries.

Most household characteristics are not associated with intimate partner violence. These characteristics include living in

Rachel Jewkes, "Intimate Partner Violence: Causes and Prevention," *The Lancet* vol. 359, April 20, 2002, pp. 1423–29. Copyright © 2002 Elsevier Limited. All rights reserved. Reproduced by permission from Elsevier.

large or crowded homes and living with in-laws. Similarly, urban or rural residence are not factors. The exception is number of children, which is frequently associated with intimate partner violence. However, in a study in Nicaragua, the first incident in almost all violent relationships occurred within a couple of years of marriage. Thus, rather than a large family causing intimate partner violence, the causation was in the reverse direction.

An influential theory explaining the relation between poverty and intimate partner violence is that it is mediated through stress. Since poverty is inherently stressful, it has been argued that intimate partner violence may result from stress.

In North America, belonging to a minority ethnic group has been thought to be associated with intimate partner violence, but associations have been largely explained by differences in education and income. Risk of intimate partner violence varies between countries and between otherwise similar settings within countries. These differences persist after adjustment for social and demographic factors, relationship characteristics, and other risk factors. Some of the difference may be explained by factors such as study design and willingness to disclose violent experience in interview settings. However, other factors also seem to be involved. Research has not been undertaken to identify exactly what these factors are. Possibly they relate to cultural differences in the status of women or acceptability of interpersonal violence. Research aimed at understanding the roots of substantial differences in prevalence between otherwise similar social settings is likely to provide important insights into the causes of violence.

Poverty Is a Key Contributor

Poverty and associated stress are key contributors to intimate partner violence. Although violence occurs in all socioeconomic groups, it is more frequent and severe in lower groups across such diverse settings as the USA, Nicaragua, and India. An influential theory explaining the relation between poverty and intimate partner violence is that it is mediated through stress. Since poverty is inherently stressful, it has been argued that intimate partner violence may result from stress, and that poorer men have fewer resources to reduce stress. However, this finding has not been supported by results from a large study of intimate partner violence in Thailand in which several sources of stress reported by men and their relation with intimate partner violence were analysed.

Research has shown the importance of levels of conflict in mediating the relation between poverty and abuse. In a study in South Africa, physical violence was not associated in the expected way with indicators of socioeconomic status including ownership of household goods, male and female occupations, and unemployment. Intriguingly, women are protected from intimate partner violence in some of the poorest households, which are those that are mainly supported by someone other than the woman or her partner (43% of all women in the study). Further analysis indicated that this form of extreme poverty reduced the scope for conflicts about household finance.

Financial independence of women is protective in some settings, but not all. Circumstances in which the woman, but not her partner, is working convey additional risk. This finding suggests that economic inequality within a context of poverty is more important than the absolute level of income or empowerment of a man or woman in a relationship. Violence is associated with the product of inequality, whether in the form of advantage to either party. Because socioeconomic injustice at a community or societal level is increasingly being shown to be important in other forms of violence, it might be important in explaining differences in prevalence of intimate partner violence, but there are no data on this factor.

Poverty, Power, and Sex Identity

Within any setting ideas vary on what it means to be a man and what constitutes successful manhood. [Richard J.] Gelles first postulated that the link between violence and poverty could be mediated through masculine identity. He argued that men living in poverty were unable to live up to their ideas of "successful" manhood and that, in the resulting climate of stress, they would hit women. Some social scientists have become especially interested in the effect of poverty on male identity and relations between male vulnerability and violence against women. They have argued that such relations are mediated through forms of crisis of masculine identity, which are often infused with ideas about honour and respect.

[Philippe] Bourgois described how Puerto Rican men growing up in New York slums feel pressurised by models of masculinity and family of their parents' and grandparents' generations, and present-day ideals of successful manhood that emphasise consumerism. Trapped in urban slums, with little or no employment, neither model of masculine success is attainable. In these circumstances, ideals of masculinity are reshaped to emphasise misogyny, substance use, and participation in crime. Violence against women becomes a social norm in which men are violent towards women they can no longer control or economically support. Violence against women is thus seen not just as an expression of male powerfulness and dominance over women, but also as being rooted in male vulnerability stemming from social expectations of manhood that are unattainable because of factors such as poverty experienced by men. Male identity is associated with experiences of power. Challenges to the exercise of power by men can be perceived by them as threats to their masculine identity. An inability to meet social expectations of successful manhood can trigger a crisis of male identity. Violence against women is a means of resolving this crisis because it allows expression of power that is otherwise denied.

Associations between intimate partner violence and situations in which husbands have lower status or fewer resources than their wives may also be substantially mediated through ideas of successful manhood and crises of male identity. The salient forms of inequality vary between settings. For example, in North America differences in education and occupational prestige convey risk, whereas in India employment differences are more important. These crossnational variations probably result from differences in cultural ideas of successful manhood. This finding shows the need for renegotiation of ideas of masculinity, and recognition of the effects of poverty and unemployment on men in prevention of intimate partner violence.

Women and Power

High levels of female empowerment seem to be protective against intimate partner violence, but power can be derived from many sources such as education, income, and community roles and not all of these convey equal protection or do so in a direct manner. In many studies, high educational attainment of women was associated with low levels of violence. The same finding has been noted for men. Education confers social empowerment via social networks, self-confidence, and an ability to use information and resources available in society, and may also translate into wealth. The relation between intimate partner violence and female education, however, is complex. In the USA and South Africa the relation has an inverted U-shape, with protection at lowest and highest educational levels.

Crosscultural research suggests that societies with stronger ideologies of male dominance have more intimate partner violence. These ideologies usually have effects at many levels within a society. At a societal level they affect, for example, female autonomy, access to political systems, influence in the economy, and participation in academic life and the arts. Such ideologies also affect laws, police, criminal justice systems, whether violence against women is criminalised, and the seriousness with which complaints from women about abuse are treated by law enforcers. At an individual level, men who hold conservative ideas about the social status of women are more likely to abuse them. Women who hold more liberal ideas are at greater risk of violence. The degree of liberality of women's ideas on their role and position is closely and positively associated with education—ie, more educated women are more liberal in these respects. The most likely explanation for the inverted U-shaped relation with education is that having some education empowers women enough to challenge certain aspects of traditional sex roles, but that such empowerment carries an increased risk of violence until a high enough level is reached for protective effects to predominate. Thus, during periods of transition in gender relations women may be at increased risk of violence.

Social support is another source of power for women. In studies from several countries, good social support was shown possibly to be protective against intimate partner violence. Temporal issues need clarification as abusive men often restrict their partner's movement and contact with others, and so abused women become isolated. This isolation is compounded by the effects of abuse on women's mental state, which can result in them withdrawing into themselves, and also by problems of compassion fatigue in those who are asked to play a supportive part. Social support during relationship problems has also been associated with increased risk of violence, but it seems likely that the explanation is that some women are more likely to discuss relationship problems when these become more severe. Notwithstanding this factor, social support, especially from a woman's family, may indicate that she is valued, enhance her self-esteem, and be a source of practical assistance during violent experiences or afterwards. Anthropological research indicates that in settings where women are valued in their own right, and the social position of single women is sufficiently high to make being unmarried or unattached a realistic option, divorce is relatively easy to obtain and women are less likely to be abused.

Ethnographic research suggests that protective effects of social empowerment extend outside the home. Women who have respect and power outside the home through community activities, including participation in microcredit schemes, are less likely to be abused than those who do not.

Relationship Conflict

The frequency of verbal disagreements and of high levels of conflict in relationships are strongly associated with physical violence. Violence is often deployed as a tactic in relationship conflict as well as being an expression of frustration or anger. Not surprisingly, marital instability—ie, a partner considering leaving the marriage—is a time of especial risk of violence. Women who leave relationships are afterwards more at risk of stalking, murder, and attempted murder.

Research on the social anthropology of alcohol drinking suggests that connections between violence and drinking and drunkenness are socially learned and not universal.

Forms of conflict especially likely to be associated with violence centre on women's transgression of conservative gender roles or challenges to male privilege, as well as matters of finance. If many sources of conflict are analysed with multiple logistic regression analysis, conflicts about transgressions of gender norms and failure to fulfill cultural stereotypes of good womanhood are among the most important variables for risk of intimate partner violence. In South India, pertinent factors include dowry disputes, female sterilisation, and not having sons, whereas factors in South Africa include women having other partners, drinking alcohol, and arguing about their partner's drinking. The differences between the variables identified reflect crosscultural differences in expected gender roles or manifestations of male privilege.

Alcohol

Alcohol consumption is associated with increased risk of all forms of interpersonal violence. Heavy alcohol consumption by men (and often women) is associated with intimate partner violence, if not consistently. Alcohol is thought to reduce inhibitions, cloud judgment, and impair ability to interpret social cues. However, biological links between alcohol and violence are complex. Research on the social anthropology of alcohol drinking suggests that connections between violence and drinking and drunkenness are socially learned and not universal. Some researchers have noted that alcohol may act as a cultural "time out" for antisocial behaviour. Thus, men are more likely to act violently when drunk because they do not feel they will be held accountable for their behaviour. In some settings, men have described using alcohol in a premeditated manner to enable them to beat their partner because they feel that this is socially expected of them. It seems likely that drugs that reduce inhibition, such as cocaine, will have similar relations to those of alcohol with intimate partner violence, but there has been little population-based research on this subject.

Social Norms

Many researchers have discussed intimate partner violence as a learned social behaviour for both men and women. The intergenerational cycling of violence has been documented in many settings. The sons of women who are beaten are more likely to beat their intimate partners and, in some settings, to have been beaten themselves as children. The daughters of women who are beaten are more likely to be beaten as adults. Women who are beaten in childhood by parents are also more likely to be abused by intimate partners as adults. Experiences of violence in the home in childhood teach children that violence is normal in certain settings. In this way, men learn to use violence and women learn to tolerate it or at least tolerate aggressive behaviour.

Crosscultural studies of intimate partner violence suggest that it is much more frequent in societies where violence is usual in conflict situations and political struggles. An example of this relation is South Africa, where not only is there a history of violent state repression and community insurrection, but also violence is deployed frequently in many situations including disputes between neighbours and colleagues at work. Verbal and physical violence between staff and patients in health settings is also very common and contributes to violence being accepted as a social norm. Many cultures condone the use of physical violence by men against women in certain circumstances and within certain boundaries of severity. In these settings, so long as boundaries are not crossed, the social cost of physical violence is low. This tolerance may result from families or communities emphasising the importance of maintenance of the male-female union at all costs, police trivialising reports of domestic strife, or lack of legislation to protect women.

Violence in Dating Relationships May Contribute to Later Domestic Abuse

Centers for Disease Control and Prevention

The Centers for Disease Control and Prevention (CDC) is the primary public health agency in the United States.

Dating violence is defined as physical, sexual, or psychological violence within a dating relationship. In a study of dating violence victimization among students in grades 7–12 during 1994–1995, the 18-month prevalence of victimization from physical and psychological dating violence was estimated at 12% and 20%, respectively. In addition to the risk for injury and death, victims of dating violence are more likely to engage in risky sexual behavior, unhealthy dieting behaviors, substance use, and suicidal ideation/attempts. Dating violence victimization can be a precursor for intimate partner violence (IPV) victimization in adulthood, most notably among women. Among adult women in the United States, an estimated 5.3 million IPV incidents occur each year, resulting in approximately 2 million injuries and 1,300 deaths. By using data from the 2003 Youth Risk Behavior Survey (YRBS), CDC [Centers for Disease Control and Prevention] analyzed the prevalence of physical dating violence (PDV) victimization among high school students and its association with five risk behaviors. The results indicated that 8.9% of students (8.9% of males and 8.8% of females) reported PDV victimization during the 12 months preceding the survey and that students reporting PDV victimization were more likely to engage in four of the five risk behaviors (i.e., sexual intercourse, attempted suicide, episodic heavy drinking, and physical

Centers for Disease Control and Prevention, "Physical Dating Violence among High School Students—United States, 2003," *Morbidity and Mortality Weekly Report* vol. 55, no. 19, May 19, 2006, pp. 532–35.

fighting). Primary prevention programs are needed to educate high school students about healthy dating relationship behaviors, and secondary prevention programs should address risk behaviors associated with dating violence victimization.

YRBS, a component of the Youth Risk Behavior Surveillance System, measures the prevalence of health risk behaviors among high school students through biennial national, state, and local surveys. The 2003 national survey obtained cross-sectional data representative of public- and private-school students in grades 9–12 in the 50 states and the District of Columbia. The overall response rate was 67%. Data from 15,214 students in 158 schools were available for analysis; 14,956 (98.3%) students answered the dating violence question. Students completed an anonymous, self-administered questionnaire that included a question about dating violence victimization. A more detailed description of these methods appears elsewhere.

PDV Victimization Highest Among Black Students

PDV victimization was defined as a response of "yes" to a single question: "During the past 12 months, did your boyfriend or girlfriend ever hit, slap, or physically hurt you on purpose?" Students were not asked whether they had had a boyfriend or girlfriend during the 12 months preceding the survey; therefore, a response of "no" might have included students who had not been dating. The following self-reported risk behaviors also were assessed: currently sexually active (had sexual intercourse with at least one person during the 3 months preceding the survey), attempted suicide (actually attempted suicide at least one time during the 12 months preceding the survey), current cigarette use (smoked cigarettes on ≥ 1 of the 30 days preceding the survey), episodic heavy drinking (had five or more alcoholic drinks in a row on ≥ 1 of the 30 days preceding the survey), and physical fighting (was in a physical fight at least one time during the 12 months preceding the survey). Specific risk behaviors were selected to represent risks that are of public health concern among high school students.

PDV victimization prevalence did not vary significantly by geographic region.

Data were weighted to produce national estimates. All calculations were performed using statistical software to account for the complex sampling design. Differences in prevalence among persons with certain characteristics were determined statistically significant if the 95% confidence intervals did not overlap. Adjusted odds ratios were calculated to examine the association between PDV victimization and the five risk behaviors using a multivariable logistic regression model that included, as predictors, the five risk behaviors and sex, grade level, race/ethnicity, and self-reported grades. In this report, data are presented for black, white, and Hispanic students; the numbers of students from other racial/ethnic populations were too small for meaningful analysis.

Among all 14,956 students, 8.9% reported experiencing PDV victimization. The prevalence of PDV victimization was similar for males (8.9%) and females (8.8%) and similar by grade level (range: 8.1%–10.1%). Prevalence of reported PDV victimization was greater among blacks (13.9%) than whites (7.0%) and Hispanics (9.3%). In addition, prevalence of PDV victimization was greater among black males (13.7%) than white males (6.6%) and higher among black females (14.0%) than white females (7.5%) and Hispanic females (9.2%). PDV victimization prevalence did not vary significantly by geographic region. Lower self-reported grades in school were associated with higher levels of PDV victimization; 6.1% of students reporting mostly A's reported PDV victimization compared with 13.7% of students receiving mostly D's or F's.

Prevalences of the five risk behaviors among all participants were as follows: currently sexually active, 34.3%; attempted suicide, 8.5%; current cigarette use, 21.9%; episodic heavy drinking, 28.3%; and physical fighting, 33.0%. After controlling for sex, grade level, race/ethnicity, self-reported grades, and the five risk behaviors examined, four of the five risk behaviors were significantly associated with PDV victimization. The only risk behavior not significantly associated with PDV victimization in the multivariable model was current cigarette use. When male and female students were analyzed separately, three of the five risk behaviors (currently sexually active, attempted suicide, and physical fighting) were significantly associated with PDV victimization in the multivariable model.

Individual and Community Poverty Contribute to Family Violence

Michael L. Benson and Greer Litton Fox

Michael L. Benson is an associate professor of criminal justice at the University of Cincinnati. Greer Litton Fox is a professor at the University of Tennessee's Department of Child and Family Studies.

Past research has explored how personality factors and the dynamics of an intimate relationship can lead to violence against women. An NIJ [National Institute of Justice] study takes a broader look at the factors at play in intimate violence. The study reveals that the incidence of violence in the home is exacerbated by economic factors apart from the characteristics of the individuals involved. Researchers found that economic problems or distresses such as losing one's job and specific circumstances such as the length of a relationship interact with the kind of community in which people live to influence the offenders and victims of intimate violence.

The study sheds light on the connections between intimate violence and personal and economic well-being and on how the type of neighborhood in which women live may influence them to stay in or leave abusive relationships. Understanding the links between these factors should help policymakers and practitioners create more targeted prevention and intervention programs and better anticipate when demand for these programs might grow. The findings suggest that service providers who help victims of violence should give priority to women in the most disadvantaged neighborhoods and address their economic circumstances.

Michael L. Benson and Greer Litton Fox, *When Violence Hits Home: How Economics and Neighborhoods Play a Role.* Washington, DC: U.S. Department of Justice, National Institute of Justice, September 2004. p. 1–6.

The Study's Findings

The study found that—

- Violence against women in intimate relationships occurred more often and was more severe in economically disadvantaged neighborhoods. Women living in disadvantaged neighborhoods were more than twice as likely to be the victims of intimate violence compared with women in more advantaged neighborhoods.

- For the individuals involved, both objective (being unemployed or not making enough money to meet family needs) and subjective (worrying about finances) forms of economic distress increase the risk of intimate violence against women.

- Women who live in economically disadvantaged communities and are struggling with money in their own relationships suffer the greatest risk of intimate violence.

- African-Americans and whites with the same economic characteristics have similar rates of intimate violence, but African-Americans have a higher overall rate of intimate violence due in part to higher levels of economic distress and location in disadvantaged neighborhoods.

The study also showed that even when measures of subjective and objective economic distress were taken into account, women living in disadvantaged neighborhoods still have higher rates of intimate violence. This may be because of the existence of many of the same social problems that increase the risk of street crime in disadvantaged neighborhoods; for example, a lower degree of social capital to respond to criminal behavior that, when longstanding, leads to a greater tolerance for deviant behavior among people living in those neighborhoods.

Effects of Economic Distress

Male job instability. Women whose male partners experienced two or more periods of unemployment over the 5-year study were almost three times as likely to be victims of intimate violence as were women whose partners were in stable jobs.

Income levels. Women living in households with high incomes experienced less violence at the hands of their intimate partners than did women whose households were less financially secure. The results showed a very consistent pattern: As the ratio of household income to needs goes up, the likelihood of violence goes down.

Financial strain. Couples who reported extensive financial strain had a rate of violence more than three times that of couples with low levels of financial strain.

Severity of violence. Women in disadvantaged neighborhoods were more likely to be victimized repeatedly or to be injured by their domestic partners than were women who lived in more advantaged neighborhoods. For instance, about 2 percent of women in advantaged neighborhoods experienced severe violence, while 6 percent of women in disadvantaged neighborhoods were the victims of severe violence.

A Volatile Mix

Researchers sought to determine whether the combination of individual economic distress and a community's economic disadvantage increases a woman's risk of intimate violence. Comparing levels of intimate violence among couples experiencing individual economic distress in both advantaged and disadvantaged neighborhoods, researchers found much higher rates of violence among couples in disadvantaged neighborhoods. The rate of intimate violence among financially distressed couples in advantaged neighborhoods is roughly half that of similarly distressed couples in disadvantaged neighborhoods. The highest rates of intimate violence are found among women who live in disadvantaged neighborhoods with men who have had high levels of job instability. In comparison, the rate of intimate violence is lowest among women whose intimate partners have stable employment and live in advantaged neighborhoods. These findings show that individual economic distress and an economically disadvantaged neighborhood work in tandem to increase a woman's risk for violence in an intimate relationship.

The stress that accompanies losing a job and seeing personal income shrink can result in severe consequences for individuals, intimate couples, and the communities in which they live.

Socioeconomics, Race, and Violence

The study found that the rate of intimate violence against women in African-American couples is about twice that for white couples. To find out why, the study looked at the relationship among economic distress, living in a disadvantaged community, and race and ethnicity. The study found that African-Americans are more likely than whites to suffer from economic distress and to live in disadvantaged neighborhoods. The study also found that the individual economic status of African-Americans and Hispanics often does not match the economic status of the neighborhoods in which they live. For instance, 36 percent of African-American couples may be considered economically disadvantaged, but more than twice as many African-Americans (77 percent) live in disadvantaged neighborhoods. Similar patterns are found for Hispanics. By contrast, white couples are much more likely to reside in neighborhoods that mirror their economic status.

To investigate this pattern further, researchers calculated the rates of intimate violence against women among African-Americans and whites while controlling separately for community disadvantage and economic distress. They found that higher rates of intimate violence among African-Americans could be accounted for by their higher levels of economic distress and their greater likelihood of living in disadvantaged neighborhoods. What's more, the rate of violence between intimate partners is virtually identical among African-Americans and whites with high incomes. However, African-Americans with low and moderate incomes do appear to have a significantly higher rate of intimate violence than whites do in those same income categories.

The study also explored the relationship between race and intimate violence by controlling for income and type of community at the same time. Results were mixed, but, in a number of cases, the difference in intimate violence between African-Americans and whites was reduced substantially. The study found that in both advantaged and disadvantaged neighborhoods, African-Americans with high incomes have rates of intimate violence that are close to or less than those for whites. Generally, when African-Americans are compared to whites with similar incomes and neighborhood economic status, the difference in the rate of intimate violence diminishes or is eliminated.

Implications for Practice

For policymakers developing effective prevention and intervention strategies, this study provides important insights into how social changes that cause economic distress influence violence against women in different racial and socioeconomic groups. The stress that accompanies losing a job and seeing personal income shrink can result in severe consequences for individuals, intimate couples, and the communities in which they live.

This study suggests to policymakers and intimate violence service providers that violence against domestic partners does not occur solely because of an offender's psychological makeup or the inability to resolve conflicts constructively in a relationship. Therefore, strategies to address intimate violence should target a broad array of potential areas for intervention and change. At the same time, law enforcement officials could use this information to deal more effectively with intimate violence in the community. Because intimate violence is more likely to occur in disadvantaged neighborhoods, this study suggests that law enforcement officials give increased attention to these neighborhoods and consider employing strategies to prevent and detect intimate partner crimes in vulnerable neighborhoods.

This study found a strong link between intimate violence and the economic well-being of couples and the communities in which they live. This means that economic practices and employment policies may play an important part in women's risk of suffering from intimate violence. It is noteworthy that, in this study, job instability and not employment status itself was a major risk factor for violence against women. The researchers suggest that when policymakers consider the problem of transitory labor demand, they could help address women's risk of intimate partner violence by giving preference to policies and practices that provide job stability rather than those that promote periodic layoffs and rehiring. The researchers also suggest that service providers may want to monitor changes in the local job force because cutbacks could potentially increase the level of intimate violence.

The study also found that the type of community in which women lived played a contributing role in their risk for intimate violence. Women experiencing economic difficulties who live in disadvantaged neighborhoods will continue to experience a greater risk for intimate violence. In light of these findings about how neighborhood types and economic distress increase the risk for intimate violence, service providers may want to consider how they develop interventions. To provide services where women at the greatest risk of intimate violence need them most, service providers could target [services for] women who live in the most disadvantaged neighborhoods.

Because economic distress has been shown to increase the risk of violence, service providers might choose to address the economic resources of these women and specifically, their need for cash assistance. Based on the findings of this study, financial assistance to women in poverty may lessen their risk of violence.

Biological Disorders Contribute to Family Violence

Colby Stong

Colby Stong is a senior editor at Neurology Reviews.

B etween 20% and 30% of all men and women in the US will be victims of domestic violence in their lifetime. Domestic violence accounts for 20% of all emergency department visits, 50% of police calls, and about 30% of murdered women. While considerable research into understanding the perpetrator's mindset has focused on learned behaviors and psychosocial issues, comparatively little effort has been devoted to exploring possible biological causes of the problem, according to David George, MD.

"Most people look at domestic violence from a psychodynamic/psychosocial perspective," said Dr. George, Section Chief of Clinical and Translational Studies at the National Institute on Alcohol Abuse and Alcoholism in Bethesda, Maryland. "These people believe that perpetrators feel inadequate and try to control other people by their behaviors, or that they grew up in homes where they were exposed to violence, and, therefore, they've learned these patterns. I was particularly interested in the fact that there has been so little emphasis given to any biological understanding of what might be taking place." Dr. George made his presentation at the 18th Annual Meeting of the American Neuropsychiatric Association [in 2007].

The first step in determining whether biological abnormalities may lead to acts of domestic violence is to closely examine who the perpetrators are, according to Dr. George. The incidence of domestic violence is approximately equal in men and women, and about 70% of perpetrators abuse alcohol, he noted. Based on interviews with several hundred people who have committed acts of domestic violence, as well as their spouses and significant others, Dr. George has observed several recurring patterns. One of these patterns is that perpetrators are likely to have been in multiple fights during their childhood. "They are going to push their teachers," noted Dr. George. "They fight with their siblings and with the kids down the street. As they grow older, most of them tend to limit their violence to the home and direct it toward their spouse or significant other."

Perpetrators also have little insight into why they become violent, and most acts of domestic violence are impulsive, said Dr. George. "There are those with a predatory side, but I do not see it often. Alcohol plays an important role in domestic violence. Alcohol is a two-edged sword. Perpetrators are going to use alcohol to calm down, but often the alcohol contributes to the likelihood of violence."

Typical behavioral symptoms in perpetrators include racing thoughts, supersensitivity to environmental stimuli, and mood swings that range from shutdown to flight, fight, and stalking. "I had one person tell me, 'If you ever got in my mind, you would probably lock me up. You would think I was crazy.' This is something that is going on inside of them," said Dr. George. "Little things are going to set them off—spilled milk at the dinner table, dirty dishes that aren't taken care of in the sink, the dinner that's late. The most interesting thing was that they feel afraid at the time of the aggression. That was very difficult for me to comprehend, because so often we are working with large and aggressive perpetrators whose victims are smaller in stature. Fear just doesn't look like it should be a significant factor."

Anxiety, Personality Disorders, and Substance Abuse

Dr. George has conducted a number of studies regarding domestic violence. One trial included perpetrators of domestic violence with alcohol dependence, nonviolent alcoholics, and healthy controls. The researchers found that violent alcoholics had a higher incidence of major depression, panic attacks, social phobia, obsessive-compulsive disorder, generalized anxiety, and certain personality disorders than did nonviolent alcoholics.

In a double-blind, placebo-controlled trial involving the administration of sodium lactate to participants, Dr. George and colleagues found that behavioral symptoms such as speech, breathing, facial grimacing, and motor activity in the arms and legs were much more accentuated in the perpetrators, as was their sense of fear, panic, and rage, compared with nonviolent controls. "These results were instrumental in changing my thinking about perpetrators of domestic violence," commented Dr. George. "It moved me from seeing them as offensive individuals to seeing them as defensive individuals. This was extremely important to me, because it directed my attention to the neuropathways that have been shown in animals to mediate defensive aggression."

Psychopathology and Fear Response

Dr. George devised a basic model for understanding the psychopathology of perpetrators of domestic violence. "Perpetrators frequently misinterpret environmental stimuli, which gives rise to a perceived sense of threat," he explained. "Sensory stimuli enter the thalamus, and from there are processed by both the cortex and the amygdala. The processing of the sensory stimuli in the amygdala is extremely fast and serves as an early warning system. The processing of the sensory stimuli in the cortex is going to be much slower and much more detailed than in the amygdala. . . . The cortex and the amygdala talk to each other. In certain situations, these sensory stimuli give rise to defensive behavior, autonomic arousal, and hypoalgesia.... If you talk to these people and ask them what it is like when they are hitting someone, they will tell you, 'It feels like my hands and arms are like feathers. I have no feeling in my hands. I don't feel as though I'm doing anything.'"

In formulating a theory for the etiology of domestic violence, Dr. George reasoned that threats trigger a conditioned fear response in perpetrators that is out of proportion to the stimulus, which may result in fear-induced aggression. "This misinterpretation arises from the abnormality in structures and pathways that mediate fear-induced aggression," he said.

In a study using PET [positron emission tomography] imaging to examine the neural structures and pathways involved in fear conditioning and fear-induced aggression, Dr. George's group found that mean CMRglc [cerebral metabolic rate for glucose] in the right hypothalamus was significantly lower in perpetrators with alcohol dependence, compared with nonviolent alcoholics and healthy controls. "At rest, when you compare the activities in the left amygdala with various cortical and subcortical structures like the thalamus and cingulate, you see a strong correlation in the nonviolent alcoholics between these structures and the amygdala, whereas in the perpetrators, you had decreased correlations," said Dr. George. "We are interpreting this to mean that the ability of the cortex to modulate the amygdala in these people is reduced. Similarly, we compared perpetrators with healthy controls. We found the same kind of finding here, decreased correlations [with the left and right amygdala]. And the nonviolent alcoholics had an increased correlation between the left thalamus and left posterior orbitofrontal cortex."

Such findings may indicate different motivations to drink alcohol for nonviolent alcoholics and alcoholic perpetrators. "Basically, we arrived at two different possibilities," Dr. George said. "The increased correlation found in nonviolent alcoholics maybe makes them more susceptible to environmental cues that trigger drinking. Whereas, I think alcoholic perpetrators are more prone, at least in the initial stages of the disease, to drink in order to decrease anxiety."

In another study, Dr. George and colleagues performed lumbar puncture in the left lateral decubitus position in alcoholic perpetrators of domestic violence, nonalcoholic perpetrators, and healthy controls. The researchers found that the nonalcoholic violent group had lower 5-HIAA (5-hydroxyindoleacetic acid) concentrations than did the other two groups, which was "not particularly surprising, given the huge literature that's out there saying that 5-HIAA is involved with impulsive types of aggression," noted Dr. George. "It is unclear as to why the alcoholics didn't have it. We then looked at testosterone, and there we found that [alcoholic perpetrators] did have higher levels of testosterone. So we have at least two neurotransmitter systems that theoretically could be involved, that could be modulating the way they process sensory information. We are looking at a number of other transmitter systems at this time."

Can Domestic Violence Be Treated?

Dr. George's current research is focusing on fMRI [functional magnetic resonance imaging], genotyping, and potential treatments. To date, he emphasized, "Treatments for domestic violence are often ineffective." In one ongoing trial, he has been comparing fluoxetine with placebo regarding their effect on measures of aggression, anxiety, and depression in those who commit acts of domestic violence. "What is really interesting is when you look at what serotonin does, it modulates sensory information," noted Dr. George.

Dr. George believes that it is possible to piece together some of these findings to understand domestic violence on the basis of a biological pathway. "This is such a primitive pathway," he commented. "Defensive aggression is present throughout the whole animal kingdom and promotes survival. With reduced cortical connection to the amygdala, perpetrators process sensory information very quickly. Based on fMRI studies, this processing of sensory information by the amygdala is out of the conscious awareness. I think that's why therapy has been so ineffective in these individuals. They are responding so quickly to sensory information that they don't even have time to think about it."

Ultimately, Dr. George believes that further studies linking conditioned fear and fear avoidance with behaviors and psychiatric diagnoses will help change the way researchers and clinicians perceive and treat perpetrators of domestic violence.

Abuse of Animals Can Signal Violence in Families

Susan I. Finkelstein

Susan I. Finkelstein is a frequent contributor to Bellwether, *the magazine of the University of Pennsylvania School of Veterinary Medicine.*

A nimals have long served as prognosticators of disease and toxins in the environment. For centuries, canaries were brought into coal mines to alert miners to carbon monoxide; if the birds died, the miners quickly evacuated. Today, scientists regard reductions and mutations in the populations of frogs and other amphibians as first signs that other species or an entire habitat might be in jeopardy.

Recently, evidence has indicated that animals can play a similar role with interpersonal violence. Psychology, sociology, and criminology studies conducted in the last quarter-century have shown that many violent offenders repeatedly committed acts of serious animal cruelty during childhood and adolescence. Other research has demonstrated consistent patterns of animal cruelty among perpetrators of common forms of violence, including child abuse, spouse abuse, and elder abuse. Recognition of these patterns may help human service professionals make life-saving decisions related to suspected instances of family violence when animal abuse is also evident.

Such was the subject of a Continuing Education course held on [the University of Pennsylvania] campus in October [2003], "Interpersonal Violence and Animal Abuse," co-sponsored by the Vet School and the School of Social Work. Jodi A. Levinthal, M.S.W., a doctoral candidate in Social Welfare at Penn, organized and led the interactive workshop, along with Phil Arkow, humane educator and chair of the Latham Foundation's Child and Family Violence Prevention Project. Ms. Levinthal is also a member of the Center for the Interaction of Animals and Society (CIAS), a multidisciplinary research center within the Vet School that provides a forum for addressing the many practical and moral issues arising from the interactions of animals and society. . . .

Recognizing the "Link"

Arkow presented striking evidence for a link between animal cruelty and human violence in the case histories of some of the twentieth century's most heinous murderers. David Berkowitz, known as "Son of Sam," shot a neighbor's Labrador retriever before committing his murders. As a child, future serial killer and cannibal Jeffrey Dahmer killed neighborhood pets and impaled animals' heads on sticks. More recently, before Columbine High School students Eric Harris and Dylan Klebold shot and killed 14 classmates and a teacher (and fatally shot themselves), they had bragged about mutilating animals to their friends.

Less dramatic but no less critical is the connection between animal abuse and family violence—"The Link," as it is called in social work circles. "Family violence often begins with pet abuse," notes Arkow. Abusive family members may threaten, injure, or kill pets, often as a way of threatening or controlling others in the family. According to the 2002 *Report of Animal Cruelty Cases* published by the Humane Society of the United States (HSUS), approximately 12 percent of the reported intentional animal cruelty cases also involved some form of family violence, including domestic violence, child abuse, spouse/child witnessing animal cruelty, or elder abuse.

Interestingly, the parent is not always the one hurting the animal. Children who abuse animals may be repeating behavior seen at home; like their parents, they too are reacting to anger or frustration with violence. Children in violent homes frequently participate in "pecking-order battering," in which they may maim or kill an animal, the only member of the household more powerless than they are. Indeed, domestic violence or neglect is the most common background for childhood cruelty to animals. Ms. Levinthal related a case in which she witnessed a child attempting to strangle a kitten during a home visit; that act led to several other revelations that ultimately confirmed her suspicions—the single mother was addicted to drugs and posed a threat to her children.

And yet, despite all the statistics, case studies, psychologists, and even FBI profilers consistently reaffirming "The Link," animal abuse crimes are not given nearly the weight in the criminal justice system that human crimes are given. In 1997, in an attempt to raise public and professional awareness about the animal cruelty/human violence connection, the HSUS created the "First Strike" campaign, which aims to strengthen collaboration among animal shelter workers, animal control officers, social service workers, law enforcement officials, veterinarians, educators, and others to establish strategies to reduce animal cruelty and family and community violence.

Authorities often discover animal abuse earlier than child or domestic abuse because it usually occurs in plain view. While hiding their own abuse, human victims may talk openly of animal abuse or neglect occurring in the family.

Indeed, professionals who help families in crisis have already begun realizing the role animals play in family violence. Many law enforcement agencies now are training officers responding to domestic violence calls how to recognize signs that a situation is life threatening: instances where the abuser has threatened suicide, is displaying a firearm, or has hurt or killed a family pet.

Creating Safe Havens for Pets and People

Additionally, domestic violence shelters, veterinarians, kennels, and local animal welfare organizations have started working together to develop "safe havens" for the pets of domestic violence victims. Many victims delay leaving the batterer out of fear for their pets' safety, but with more than 100 Safe Haven for Pets programs now operating around the country, many domestic violence victims no longer have to choose between their well-being and their pets. Under the various programs, shelters actually house the pets with their owners on a temporary basis, find space for the animals at local kennels, or recruit volunteers to act as "foster parents" for the endangered pets while their owners seek medical attention, counseling, and other help.

Increasing awareness levels have indeed made a difference in the past ten years: the evidence that cruelty toward animals is indicative of other violent behaviors has been so overwhelming that 41 states and the District of Columbia currently have felony-level convictions for serious acts of animal abuse. Still, some law enforcement officials and social service workers say that putting greater emphasis on animal abuse is impractical, given all the other crimes and cases they must respectively handle. "Animal abuse must be redefined as a crime of violence rather than a crime against property," counters Arkow. "It must be perceived and documented as a human welfare issue. The network of community caregivers must be cross-trained to recognize and report all forms of violence."

Authorities often discover animal abuse earlier than child or domestic abuse because it usually occurs in plain view. While hiding their own abuse, human victims may talk openly of animal abuse or neglect occurring in the family. Since legislation governing animal abuse and child abuse investigation and intervention are different, animal control agents often enter homes when social service workers cannot. Working together through cross-reporting, these agencies can help each other gain information about abusive situations and end cycles of violence that often have tragic results.

Immigrant Status Affects Victim Reporting of Domestic Violence

Edna Erez and Carolyn Copps Hartley

Edna Erez is a professor of justice studies and a research associate at Kent State University's Institute for the Study and Prevention of Violence. Carolyn Copps Hartley is an assistant professor at the University of Iowa's School of Social Work.

The immigration context of battered immigrant women presents unique and intricate problems vis a vis the justice system. It involves a complex set of interacting cultural, legal, and practical concerns, making immigrant women remain in battering relationships, reluctant to report their abuse, and unwilling to participate in justice proceedings.

Battered immigrant women are often economically dependent and financially insecure. They frequently do not have linguistic and occupational skills or gainful employment, and they view their primary role as that of wives and mothers. The husband is the breadwinner who typically conducts all communication with the outside world. Immigrant women commonly rely on their husbands, regardless of how abusive they are, as their sole means of support.

Battered immigrant women are highly isolated due to their immigration circumstances. In the new country they often lack extended family (e.g., parents, siblings) or other support networks. Immigrant women often move to follow their husbands, leaving behind their own familial and social support systems. Furthermore, immigrant women often live with or are close to their husbands' families due to cultural dictates

Edna Erez and Carolyn Copps Hartley, "Battered Immigrant Women and the Legal System: A Therapeutic Jurisprudence Perspective," *Western Criminology Review*, vol. 4, no. 2, 2003, pp. 155–69. Copyright © 1998–2007, Western Criminology Review. All rights reserved. Reproduced by permission of WCR/CJ Development Fund.

and economic considerations. Proximity to the husband's family leads not only to increased support for the abuse, but also to increased likelihood of abuse by in-laws.

The Stigma of Divorce

Despite severe and extended abuse, battered immigrant women tend to remain in abusive relationships for a long time. There are social pressures on all women to remain in a marriage. In some cultures, however, divorce leaves such a stigma that a divorced woman may never be accepted by her cultural community or may never be able to remarry. In cultures where lineage, family integrity, and strict adherence to role obligation are highly valued, the risk of disgrace or losing face is serious enough to prevent a woman from leaving. Further, memberships in churches, mosques, temples, or other religious institutions provide women an amplified sense of community, much needed continuity, and support. At the same time, cultural norms and religious prescriptions may not offer battered women the kind of support and encouragement they need to escape from violence in the home.

If the woman leaves, she is typically deemed responsible for the end of the marriage even if she has been abused. Her family of origin oftentimes will not accept her back, because such an act brings shame and disgrace on the family name and mars the collective perception of the family's honor. Research confirms the experiences of counselors and social workers that work with minority or immigrant women: families will not support a battered woman's decision to leave, even if she has suffered serious injuries. In many cases, the women fear retaliation by their husbands' families (and sometimes their own families) if they return to their country of origin. Leaving an abuser to return to the home country also presents the women with tremendous difficulties in terms of providing economic support for themselves and their children. In many countries, gender is a barrier to adequate employment. Women who leave their husbands are commonly subjected to severe stigma and isolation, endure significant economic hardship, and have very low chances of a remarriage.

Religious values and institutions often reinforce traditional responses to woman battering and act as disincentives to reveal the abuse or contact the justice system.

Immigrant women themselves feel they must live up to their roles as wives and mothers, demanding the sacrifice of personal autonomy and freedom. They have well internalized traditional expectations and the cultural modeling of appropriate social behavior. As a woman is considered the pivotal point of the family, regardless of the physical or verbal abuse she may endure, her primary responsibilities are to care for and safeguard her family and steadfastly remain at her husband's side. The ideal of a "good wife" is strongly linked to its antithetical notion of the "shameful wife"—one who violates normative expectations, such as revealing the abuse or leaving the abuser. The "shameful wife" image acts as powerful self-discipline, militating against abused women's attempts to disclose the violence or leave their abuser. Proscription to reveal to outsiders unbecoming or improper behavior of family members (whether from their children or from their husbands) is also included within the cultural script for many immigrant women.

Many Reasons to Endure the Abuse

Leaving her husband usually also means relinquishing both financial resources (such as her home and personal effects) and vital practical services she needs to obtain work or maintain her job. These services include childcare, which is commonly provided by her extended family or by her community. Immigrant women's social relationships are also often confined to those who share their language. Lack of linguistic skills thus contributes to the isolation of immigrant women, maintaining their dependence on the family, which in turn reinforces familial and cultural interpretations of assault. Members of the linguistic community are often linked to the husband and, thus, unlikely to support the woman against him.

Although there are many positive and practical aspects of extended families, in circumstances of abuse its very self-sufficiency paradoxically works against the needs of battered women.

Immigration also negatively affects immigrant communities' predilection to exposing abuse in their midst for fear of directing attention to their community. This tendency for secrecy and denial of abuse results in a weaker system of supports and aid for abused immigrant women, who in the same situations may have received assistance in their home communities. Attempts to raise issues of violence against women in immigrant communities are often deflected by the community leadership as an imposition of irrelevant "Western" agendas, and insistence that "our tradition" or "our families" do not suffer from these problems which are endemic to "Western" marriages. Religious leaders in many immigrant communities are quick to point out that women who disclose domestic violence are a very small contingent of "deviant, rebellious women," and that abuse does not really occur among their followers. Religious values and institutions often reinforce traditional responses to woman battering and act as disincentives to reveal the abuse or contact the justice system.

Immigrant Battered Women and Reporting the Violence

Immigrant victims in general, and battered immigrant women in particular, are reluctant to report crime and cooperate with authorities due to an intricate combination of cultural, social, and legal reasons. Within immigrant communities there is a preference to treat interpersonal conflicts as private matters to be resolved internally, even in the extended family network. Immigrant battered women therefore exhibit strong reluctance to reveal the abuse to social service agencies, religious leaders, or any outside family members as it will bring shame upon themselves, their husbands, and their children.

A woman who violates social and gender norms may also be disowned by her family and harassed by her community. Although there are many positive and practical aspects of extended families, in circumstances of abuse its very self-sufficiency paradoxically works against the needs of battered women. Fears of being shunned by her family or ostracized by her community are among the strongest inhibitors of reporting violence to officials. Appeals for help to outsiders (including police and social or welfare agents) are therefore not perceived as an option for many battered immigrant women.

Some battered immigrant women are afraid that official action will lead to the deportation of their abusers, which they believe could mean loss of their own dependent immigrant status.

Immigrant women often do not know that battering is a criminal offense in their new country, nor are they aware of any social, legal, health, or other services available for women in their predicament. If they do recognize the battering as a criminal offense, immigrant women are reluctant to call the police. In addition to aversion from involving outsiders in private family affairs, prior negative experiences with the police and the justice system in their own countries often color battered women's willingness to call the police for help in their new country.

The overriding rationale for many immigrant women to stay in abusive relationships and to not report their battering is the prospect of losing their children. More specifically, many immigrant women fear that deportation or loss of resident status will lead to their losing legal custody of their children. In fact, return to their own country often means never seeing their children again and loss of custody rights in favor of the father. Battered immigrant women sometimes believe, often because their abusers have told them so, that separation or divorce in the host country will have the same result. In the U.S., however, the contrary is often the case, as the courts are likely to award custody to the non-abusive parent even when she does not have legal immigration status.

Fear of Law Enforcement Agencies

Immigrant women who have managed to overcome cultural incentives to remain silent are still wary of requesting help from law enforcement agencies. They may have had negative experiences with authorities in their country of origin or fear unpleasant experiences with legal institutions in their new country. They may also hold legitimate concerns that they will be subjected to differential treatment because of their ethnicity, gender, and immigration status. Language and communication barriers further add to their reluctance to contact the justice system.

Some battered immigrant women are afraid that official action will lead to the deportation of their abusers, which they believe could mean loss of their own dependent immigrant status. Few women are aware of recent U.S. laws that can offer many abused immigrants an avenue to attain legal immigration status independent of their abusers through the Violence Against Women Act (VAWA). Deportation is an omnipresent weapon for abusers to threaten their immigrant partners, regardless of their partners' immigration status. Batterers often use lawful immigration status to intimidate and coerce their partners to stay or comply with their demands. Abusers of undocumented immigrant women routinely threaten to call immigration authorities if the victim reports the abuse. Even for documented women, the threat of deportation is powerful enough to prevent them from leaving. Distrust of the government, ignorance of immigration law, and deception by abusers often combine to keep immigrant women in abusive relationships and prevent them from reporting the battering.

> *For undocumented women, leaving is more difficult, because without immigration papers they cannot work legally and, in the U.S., may not be entitled to welfare assistance, including housing.*

More informed abused immigrant women sometimes hesitate to call authorities because they are afraid that the batterer's probable arrest record resulting from reporting the abuse may hinder his attempts to gain lawful immigration status. Current criminal justice practices, expressed in many states' laws concerning mandatory or presumed arrest, have been challenged by feminists and advocates of all battered women, but they have been particularly criticized as harmful to battered immigrant women. Battered women who call the police often do not want to have the abusers arrested, as they are economically and/or emotionally dependent on them. They merely want to stop the violence. Arrest of the batterer is an even less desirable outcome for immigrant battered women who believe that they are dependent on their abuser for their immigration status. Further, the dual arrest practices that often take place under mandatory/presumed arrest policies (i.e. police arresting both the perpetrator and the female victim rather than the primary aggressor) may result in a criminal record for the parties, which in turn may adversely affect prospects for immigration status adjustment and related outcomes.

Isolation and Language Barriers

Access to information has always been a major factor imped-ing women's utilization of appropriate support services or ap-peals to justice. Through their employment and education op-portunities, men are more likely to have superior language skills and better access to information. Typically, it is the man who negotiates family affairs with the outside world. As the primary conduit of information to the women in the house-hold, men can maintain control, and this power is often a part of the domination characteristic of abusive relationships. Further, the control tactics abusers often use against their im-migrant wives exploit and perpetuate the very same vulner-abilities that immigrant women need to overcome in order to escape the abuse and end their isolation or dependency on the abusers.

For recently arrived immigrant women, the language bar-riers exacerbate their isolation. Inability to communicate has been a major obstacle when police are called to the house by concerned relatives or neighbors. Frequently, immigrant women are pre-literate in their own language. An inability to read, combined with other language problems, reinforces bar-riers to accessing information and communicating effectively. Lack of fluency in the mainstream language precludes useful searches for information on remedies, resources, and services available through the justice and health care systems. For un-documented women, leaving is more difficult, because with-out immigration papers they cannot work legally and, in the U.S., may not be entitled to welfare assistance, including hous-ing. Few know, for instance, that if they qualify for immigra-tion benefits in the U.S. because they have been abused by a citizen or legal resident spouse, they can receive permission from the INS to access the welfare safety net. Nor do they know that their citizen children can receive benefits even if the mother cannot.

CHAPTER 3

Is Domestic Violence a Gender Issue?

Chapter Preface

At one time it was assumed that all victims of family violence were women and children. Pop culture images of women striking men—chasing after their deadbeat husbands with rolling pins and frying pans, for example—were common and treated with humor. In the classic 1949 battle-of-the-sexes film *Adam's Rib*, starring Katherine Hepburn and Spencer Tracy, a housewife goes on trial for trying to kill her cheating husband. Judy Holliday was nominated for a Golden Globe award for her portrayal of the ditzy, spurned wife, who, when asked on the witness stand how she felt after shooting her husband, replies, "Hungry!"

Domestic violence in real life is, of course, no laughing matter. The gravity of the issue became widely known in the 1970s, when it was taken up by the burgeoning modern women's movement. For two decades the prevailing paradigm in the field of family violence studies held that men were inherently prone to commit violence against women, and that they needed to be rehabilitated or incarcerated—or both. Subsumed into the larger category of "violence against women," domestic abuse as a complex and dangerous dynamic between two volatile personalities became lost in the rhetoric of feminism, according to some observers. Early studies by family violence experts Murray Straus and Richard Gelles, however, found that women were nearly as likely to hit their male partners or to hit back when they were struck first.

Other researchers balked, though, arguing that, by and large, only men inflict a state of "terror" on their intimate partners, whereas women tend to attack in reaction to being harmed. Patricia Tjaden, the author of a study on the subject for the Center for Policy Research in Denver, Colorado, has questioned the "mutual-abuse" argument: "Where are all the male victims?" she wondered, adding that only women are victims of "systematic terrorism." Complicating matters even more is the difficulty of ensuring consistent and effective research methodologies to come up with clear answers. Different kinds of research surveys yield different statistics.

Women are, however, known to sustain more injuries than men do in violent encounters with their partners—or, at any rate, they report their injuries more often. Family conflict researcher M.J. George has called domestic violence against men "the great taboo" because male victims may be even more secretive and ashamed than female victims, refusing to report or seek care for injuries for fear of being thought of as less than manly. When professional baseball player Chuck Finley filed for divorce from his wife, the former model Tawny Kitaen, amidst allegations that his wife physically assaulted him, the world wondered how a woman could possibly batter a six-and-a-half-foot-tall professional athlete. Many experts have concluded that violence is not gender-specific, as previously believed. The essays in this chapter explore the differences in male and female intimate partner violence, focusing on the many nuances of the problem.

Men's Violence Is Intended to Inflict Terror in Women

Michael P. Johnson

Michael P. Johnson is an associate professor of sociology, women's studies, and African and African American studies at Pennsylvania State University.

Ever since Suzanne Steinmetz's 1977–1978 article on "battered husbands," we have been hearing this lament—that the feminists are wrong, that women are as violent as men, that domestic violence is not about gender or patriarchy. As [David M.] Fergusson, [L. John] Horwood, and [Elizabeth M.] Ridder put it, their work "suggest[s] the need for a broadening of perspective in the field of domestic violence away from the view that domestic violence is usually a gender issue involving male perpetrators and female victims and toward the view that domestic violence most commonly involves violent couples who engage in mutual acts of aggression."

I want to make four major points in my response to the Fergusson, Horwood, and Ridder article, points that are equally relevant to other articles like it that continue to appear in our journals and in the general media suggesting that women are as violent as men in intimate relationships. First, there are three major types of intimate partner violence, only one of which is the kind of violence that we all think of when we hear the term "domestic violence." Second, that type of intimate partner violence is, indeed, primarily male perpetrated and is most definitely a gender issue. Third, Fergusson, Horwood, and Ridder's article is *not* about that type of violence. In fact, it is hardly about violence at all. Fourth, serious errors

Michael P. Johnson, "Domestic Violence: It's Not about Gender—Or Is It?" *Journal of Marriage and Family* vol. 67, no. 5, December 2005, pp. 1126–30. Copyright © 2005 National Council on Family Relations. Reproduced by permission of Blackwell Publishers on behalf of National Council on Family Relations.

of fact, theory, and intervention inevitably follow from the failure to acknowledge the major differences among the three types of intimate partner violence.

Three Types of Intimate Partner Violence

A growing segment of the domestic violence literature demonstrates that there is more than one type of intimate partner violence. I first presented this theoretical and conceptual argument at professional meetings in the early 1990s, with publications beginning to appear in 1995. Since that time, I have continued to present and publish papers that document the differences among major types of intimate partner violence, types that must not be conflated lest we make serious mistakes in our research, and in the policy recommendations that may follow from it.

Although all three types of intimate partner violence can be either frequent or infrequent . . . and can range from relatively minor acts of violence to homicidal assaults, intimate terrorism is the type most likely to be frequent and brutal.

The importance of making such distinctions is also supported by other scholars' publications, some of which build upon my framework, others of which come to the same conclusion from other perspectives. It is no longer scientifically or ethically acceptable to speak of domestic violence without specifying, loudly and clearly, the type of violence to which we refer.

In my control-based typology of intimate partner violence, the three major types are distinguished from each other by the control context within which they are embedded. Control context is conceptualized at the level of the relationship rather than the immediate situation and is based on non-situation-specific dyadic information about the controlling and violent behaviors of both partners in the relationship. Briefly, the three types are (a) violence enacted in the service of taking general control over one's partner (*intimate terrorism*), (b) violence utilized in response to intimate terrorism (*violent resistance*), and (c) violence that is not embedded in a general pattern of power and control but is a function of the escalation of a specific conflict or series of conflicts (*situational couple violence*). As I do not plan to say much about violent resistance in this comment, I want to point out here that I purposely do not use the term *self-defense*. Violent resistance to intimate terrorism does not necessarily meet the legal definition of self-defense, and it is not always seen as self-defense by the women who respond violently to their partner's intimate terrorism. Thus, a question asking whether the violence was enacted in self-defense cannot identify violent resistance.

If we do not operationalize distinctions among the types of intimate partner violence, and instead simply make generalizations about domestic violence from . . . biased samples, we create serious misconceptions.

Although all three types of intimate partner violence can be either frequent or infrequent (within a relationship), and can range from relatively minor acts of violence to homicidal assaults, intimate terrorism is the type most likely to be frequent and brutal. Furthermore, it is the type that people bring to mind when they hear the term *domestic violence*. I am certainly aware that as scientists we can and do operationalize domestic violence quite precisely (although not necessarily consistently). Nevertheless, the term *domestic violence* carries real baggage with it that may not correspond to our operationalizations. When folks settle down to watch a movie on domestic violence, read a book about it, or critique a journal article analyzing it, they expect to learn about relationships in which controlling violence is a central feature. Thus, no matter how careful we are about spelling out our operationalization of domestic violence, we and our readers routinely fall into the trap of thinking that our conclusions apply to the prototype of domestic violence—intimate terrorism. Sometimes I wish we could abandon the term *domestic violence* altogether.

The problem is exacerbated by the fact that our common sampling designs are heavily biased with regard to these different types of intimate partner violence. On the one hand, agency samples gathered from shelters, hospitals, police records, or the courts are biased heavily in favor of intimate terrorism because intimate terrorism is the type of violence that is most likely to be repetitive and to escalate, thereby producing incidents that draw the attention of neighbors, injuries that lead to hospital visits, and terror that leads the victim to seek help from the police, shelters, or courts. On the other hand, general samples, such as the one used in the Fergusson, Horwood, and Ridder article, are heavily biased in favor of situational couple violence. These so-called random samples are dominated by situational couple violence for two reasons: (a) because situational couple violence is the most common type of intimate partner violence and (b) because refusals further reduce the number of victims or perpetrators of intimate terrorism who are interviewed.

Looking at men only [M.P.] Johnson, using 1970s Pittsburgh data, found that the violence in a general sample was only 11% intimate terrorism, in a court sample was 68% intimate terrorism, and in a shelter sample was 79% intimate terrorism. Similarly, [Nicola] Graham-Kevan and [John] Archer, using 2002 British data, found that the violence in a general sample was 33% intimate terrorism, whereas that in a shelter sample was 88% intimate terrorism.

If we do not operationalize distinctions among the types of intimate partner violence, and instead simply make generalizations about domestic violence from such biased samples, we create serious misconceptions. For example, feminist scholars make this mistake when we use numbers derived from general surveys to describe the extent of violence against women, such as that 50% of marriages involve domestic violence. We and our audiences think that we are speaking about intimate terrorism, whereas the numbers refer to situational couple violence, which is much more common than intimate terrorism. Another example is the current case, in which the authors make statements about domestic violence, implying intimate terrorism, when at best they have information about situational couple violence. I say "at best" because it appears to me that their findings actually have little to do with violence at all, let alone with intimate terrorism. I have more to say about this later, but first let me speak briefly to the general evidence on the gender issue.

Although situational couple violence is nearly gender symmetric and not strongly related to gender attitudes, intimate terrorism (domestic violence) is almost entirely male perpetrated and is strongly related to gender attitudes.

Intimate Terrorism Is Primarily Male Perpetrated

There are two types of evidence regarding the relationship between gender and the different types of intimate partner violence. First, there is indirect evidence derived from over 25 years of research that has not operationalized distinctions among the types of intimate partner violence. This evidence is indirect because it involves the comparison of findings from general survey samples that are biased in favor of situational couple violence with those from agency samples that are biased in favor of intimate terrorism. Second, there is direct evidence from the relatively small number of more recent studies that have actually operationalized the distinctions.

The most comprehensive indirect evidence comes from Archer's meta-analysis, in which he found that intimate partner violence in agency samples was heavily male perpetrated, whereas that in general samples was roughly gender symmetric. Direct evidence comes from Johnson's finding that 97% of the intimate terrorism in a 1970s Pittsburgh sample was male perpetrated, compared with 56% of the situational couple violence. Other direct evidence comes from Graham-Kevan and Archer, who found in Britain that 87% of intimate terrorism was male perpetrated, compared with 45% of situational couple violence.

Another indicator of the relevance of gender is the relationship of intimate partner violence to traditional gender attitudes and misogyny. A summary of some of the indirect evidence can be found in [David B.] Sugarman and [S.L.] Frankel's (1996) meta-analysis that found a strong relationship between traditional gender attitudes and male-perpetrated intimate partner violence in agency samples, a weak relationship in general samples. Direct evidence comes from [Amy] Holtzworth-Munroe's work, in which she finds that male perpetrators of intimate terrorism have significantly more misogynistic attitudes than do nonviolent men, whereas perpetrators of situational couple violence have the same attitudes toward women as do nonviolent men.

Thus, although situational couple violence is nearly gender symmetric and not strongly related to gender attitudes, intimate terrorism (domestic violence) is almost entirely male perpetrated and is strongly related to gender attitudes.

An Analysis

A careful analysis of Fergusson, Horwood, and Ridder's operationalization of domestic violence suggests that not only is this article not about intimate terrorism, it is hardly even about violence. . . .

It appears that although the authors use the term *domestic violence* more than 145 times in this article, and they shock us with their report that "domestic conflict was present in 70% of the relationships," in fact only about 17% of the relationships involved any violence at all and perhaps 2%–5% involved violence that produced injury or fear. This article is certainly not about intimate terrorism, a form of violence that has been shown in study after study to produce both fear and injury. It is hardly even an article about situational couple violence. It is essentially an article about the effects of all the nonviolent aggressive behaviors in a scale that is labeled as violence victimization, behaviors such as "cursed or sworn at you," "stomped off during a disagreement," "called you fat, ugly, or unattractive," and "accused you of being a lousy lover." This article has nothing to tell us about policies regarding the domestic violence faced by the terrorized women encountered in our emergency rooms, police stations, courts, and shelters, women who have in almost all cases experienced not only fear, but terror, not only injury, but repeated and often severe injury.

Errors of Fact, Theory, and Intervention

Errors of fact follow from the failure to make distinctions among types of violence. Currently, the best known examples are related to the gender debate initiated by [Suzanne K.] Steinmetz's (1977–1978) argument that there are as many battered husbands as there are battered wives. In fact, only situational couple violence, not intimate terrorism, is gender symmetric. Her mistake has been perpetuated through almost 30 years of sometimes acrimonious scholarly debate, right up to the current case.

Similar errors will probably be found with respect to many other areas of knowledge about intimate partner violence. For example, although a major meta-analysis on so-called intergenerational transmission of violence finds a generally weak relationship between childhood experiences of family violence and adult perpetration of domestic violence, a more careful look at the results suggests that there is a weak relationship only for general survey studies (situational couple violence) and a moderate relationship for agency studies (intimate terrorism).

Furthermore, such errors of fact lead to errors of theory. In the gender debate, feminist theorists working primarily with agency samples that are dominated by intimate terrorism argue that gender theory or control theory must be the major sources of insight into the nature of domestic violence. Family violence theorists, working with samples dominated by situational couple violence, argue that theories of interpersonal conflict must be central. The recognition that these two groups of theorists are trying to explain different phenomena provides a simple approach to the theoretical impasse: different theories for different types of violence.

My intention is not to justify or minimize women's violence but to recognize it for what it is (mostly situational couple violence or violent resistance) and to design our theories and interventions appropriately.

Finally, errors of theory lead to potentially life-threatening errors of intervention strategy and general policy. In Fergusson, Horwood, and Ridder's article, for example, a study of situational couple violence (to the extent that it is about any violence at all) is presented as the basis for recommendations about policies that would be applied primarily to intimate terrorism. In spite of the authors' statement that "[t]hese findings are to some extent consistent with conclusions drawn by Johnson and Ferraro (2000), who believe that there are multiple forms of domestic violence," they end by recommending shifts in our policies that would essentially treat those who enter our medical, social service, and criminal justice systems as if they were involved in situational couple violence, asking the couples to "work together to harmonize their relationships."

There is a good reason why feminists do not recommend such an approach. Women who come into contact with these agencies are in most cases dealing with intimate terrorism, not situational couple violence. We would be asking women who are terrorized by their partners to go into a counseling situation that calls for honesty. We would actually encourage them to tell the truth to a partner who in many cases has beaten them severely in response to criticism and who might well murder them in response to their attempt to "harmonize."

The Gender Issue

With regard to the gender issue, we can conclude that we have yet another study that suggests that situational couple violence is roughly gender symmetric. We need to remember, however, that this "symmetry" is a special kind, referring merely to the fact that as many women as men have committed at least one of the "violent" acts included in the scale, at least once in the past year. It does not follow that what we have is primarily "mutual acts of aggression," for two reasons: (a) We have no data on frequency and (b) even if the frequency of violence were the same for men and women, it would not follow that the violent acts occurred during the same events. And of course, in this study, as in virtually all others in which we have the relevant data, even situational couple violence is asymmetric in the sense that men's violence produces more frequent and more severe injuries, thereby producing a fear (or even terror) that is quite rare when women are violent toward their male partners. My intention is not to justify or minimize women's violence but to recognize it for what it is (mostly situational couple violence or violent resistance) and to design our theories and interventions appropriately.

On the central issue of this article, the effect of intimate abuse on mental health, the data speak loudly to the power of partner abuse. Even with a measure of so-called violence victimization that in this sample includes very little violence, the authors are able to demonstrate effects on a variety of mental health outcomes. As one of the anonymous reviewers of this comment put it, "There *are* harmful effects of psychological abuse. . . . Caustic, cruel forms of communication are corrosive to relationships and to personal well-being." Imagine how much stronger Fergusson et al.'s findings would have been had they actually operationalized intimate terrorism/domestic violence.

Male Violence Is Fundamentally Different from Female Violence

Kerrie James

Kerrie James is the clinical director of Relationships Australia, a nonprofit relationship support and counseling service with offices throughout Australia.

Debates about the prevalence of women's violence towards their male partners continue to provoke controversy in the literature and media. Practitioners are often confronted with claims such as 'she is the violent one' or 'it was mutual violence'. The controversy arises not only from men who claim to be victims of women's violence, but from the conflicting outcomes of research studies, some of which indicate equal rates of perpetration of physical abuse by men and women, and others showing much higher incidence of violence by men. In addition, comparison of studies is difficult because of differing definitions of violence, methodologies and samples.

In my previous paper, 'Truth or Fiction: Men as Victims of Domestic Violence?' I argued that although women do commit 'intimate partner violence' (IPV) towards male partners, their violence is not equivalent to men's violence either in intent, frequency, severity or outcome. In this paper, I will review the research that has been conducted since that paper was written, to see if those claims are still current.

I will first address the relative incidence of male versus female IPV; secondly, the relative severity of violence committed

Kerrie James, "Understanding Men's Versus Women's Intimate Partner Violence," Australian Government Office for Women, Department of Families, Housing, Community Services and Indigenous Affairs, Partnerships against Domestic Violence 2, Commonwealth Government of Australia, 2004. Funded by Partnerships Against Domestic Violence 2, an initiative of the Commonwealth Government of Australia, and commissioned by Relationships Australia, SA. Reproduced by permission.

by men and women; thirdly, the meaning of violent acts, including intentions of each gender and the relationship context in which violence occurs.

Incidence of Male Versus Female Intimate Partner Violence

Some studies have found that women are equally violent in heterosexual partnerships. A meta-analytic review, which examined 82 studies comparing male and female violence, found that women appear as 'likely or slightly more likely than men to use physical aggression during conflicts with an intimate partner' [John Archer cited in a 2004 article by Kris Henning and Lynette Feder]. These studies are mostly based on community surveys using the Conflict Tactics Scale (CTS or CTS2), which asks subjects about their use of violence, and their partner's use of violence. Many of the studies that report equal use of violence by men and women used the Conflict Tactics Scale to measure the perpetration of violent acts. This scale has been criticised for:

- not considering the context and consequences of violence

- not addressing sexual aggression

- not taking account of motivations for aggression, such as self-defence

- not taking account of the wider historical context of the relationship.

[Murray A.] Straus developed the revised CTS2 that addressed some of these concerns. A study of college students using the CTS2 still found that

- males and females committed physical aggression at equal rates

- that women were more psychologically abusive

- that women who physically aggress are not always acting out of self-defence

- and that women do sexually coerce men, but, unlike men who sexually coerce, do not use physical abuse or intimidation to engage in unwanted sex.

Studies of incidence of IPV by gender have been criticised for bias, particularly those that use the CTS in the context of telephone surveys. Criticisms include the following:

1. *Framing of questions*: In studies that use CTS, or the revised CTS 2, the questions about violence are framed in terms of *normal* disagreements, annoyances etc. within which violence might erupt. This might steer people to only report on violence in relation to conflict, as opposed to violence that occurs not in a context of conflict. Such phrasing of questions could lead to over-reporting of violence, making it look more equal than it is.

2. *Comparing different samples*: Studies appear to be comparing different samples, one from the general community and the other from 'help seeking' or clinical settings. 'Studies with shelter samples, for example, include physical aggression by women but much higher rates by men; community samples, on the other hand, tend to show about equal rates of aggression' [John Archer, 2000, cited in D. Saunders, 2002].

Community samples have led to the use of the term 'family violence' to imply that men and women are equally likely to be both perpetrators and victims of less serious IPV, as compared to clinical samples, where men are more likely to be perpetrators of violence that is more severe. In clinical samples, women are overwhelmingly represented as litigants in legal procedures, in refuges and in medical/hospital settings as victims of men's domestic violence. Straus found that men's average frequency of assaults against partners was 21% greater than the frequency of such assaults by women, and 42% greater for severe assaults. In a recent study [2004] by [Steve]

Basile, the ratio was 10 to 1, and in another it was 5 to 1. These researchers argue that men do not come forward to apply for protection orders because of institutional and cultural constraints, particularly men's reluctance to seek help. However, it has also been estimated that 20% of women do not report partner violence or seek medical help because of shame and fear.

3. *The issue of 'lying' or under/over-reporting*: Studies relying on men's testimony of their own and partner violence typically find that men under-report, lie or minimise their own violence while 'there is a tendency for women to downplay the effect of violence used against them' [D.H. Currie, cited in Henning and Feder's 2004 study].

4. *Context of questions*: The National Violence Against Women Survey, which interviewed 8,000 men and 8,000 women, used a range of measures to assess subjects' victimization in IPV. This produced a much greater discrepancy between the genders with women being victims of violence at a much greater rate than men. Interestingly, the investigators asked only about victimization, not their experience of perpetrating violence. Asking about victimization and perpetration leads people to compare themselves with their partner, and perhaps balance the ledger by focusing on the other's wrongs. In other words, if researchers only ask about being victimized, people are able to honestly report on this, without having to weigh up who is the worst offender.

Violence in lesbian relationships, and the abuse perpetrated by women towards dependent children, speaks of the capacity of women for physical violence.

This study avoids the methodological problems of solely relying on the CTS, and stands up to rigorous scientific methods including substantial sample size and sampling techniques. Although, like other surveys, it taps the community sample, it does reveal a significant difference in perpetration of violence with men being the major perpetrators.

> The study found that women were significantly more likely than men to report being victimized by a current or former marital/opposite-sex cohabitating partner, whether the time period considered was the individual's lifetime or the 12 months preceding the survey, and whether the type of violence considered was rape, physical assault, or stalking.... Women were 22.5 times more likely to report being raped, 2.9 times more likely to report being physically assaulted, and 8.2 times more likely to report being stalked by a current or former marital/opposite-sex cohabiting partner at some time in their lives. In addition the average frequency of victimization was significantly greater for women than men.

This study gives much wanted clarity to the debate, confirming that men's violence occurs more frequently. This is not to assert, however, that women's violence and aggression towards men does not exist. Violence in lesbian relationships, and the abuse perpetrated by women towards dependent children, speaks of the capacity of women for physical violence. Women certainly report themselves as being violent in a number of studies, so it is not just a matter of men unfairly accusing women of violence towards them.

However, overall men appear to perpetrate IPV at a greater rate than women, and they are far more likely to cause serious injury. The rates of serious injury suffered by women as measured by women presenting at legal and medical services remains at a much higher level than that for men. In some places in the USA, 'pro-arrest' policies mean that women are being arrested for domestic violence at the same rate as men, if both have been involved in IPV, regardless of who has been more seriously injured, or who initiated the violence, or who has the greatest history of violence.

This leads to a consideration of the differences in gender of type of violence and severity of injuries.

Severity of Violence

Although many more women victims of IPV apply for some kind of help, the studies by Basile and [J.] McFarlane found that the alleged violence of both male and female perpetrators was similar in type and severity. These authors argue that women's violence is therefore as serious as men's and should be taken as seriously. Basile, in his study of litigants in domestic assault cases, which included same sex couples, found that overall, females were more psychologically abusive and equally physically assaultive. The significant difference was that male defendants were more likely to use sexual coercion. This study used the revised CTS2 to analyse affidavits submitted to the courts describing the violence the plaintiff felt warranted protection.

However, other studies conclude that the most serious violence is more likely to be perpetrated by men. In a meta-analysis of over 80 studies, Archer found that while women were slightly more likely than men to use one or more acts of physical aggression and to use such acts more frequently, men were more likely to inflict an injury. Overall, 62% of those injured by a partner were women. Other studies have looked at applicants for protection orders, and have compared the type and severity of violence alleged by both male and female victims. [H.] Melton and [J.] Belknap report that men were more likely than women to use pushing, grabbing, shoving, dragging and strangling, whereas women were more likely to use hitting with or throwing an object and biting the victim. The National Violence Against Women Survey, 1995, found a 42% injury rate for women, and 19% for men. A large number of studies have found that males are more likely to inflict injury. As violence gets more severe, women sustain more serious injuries and at a greater rate than do men. Studies have also failed to include or identify separating and divorcing couples where the rates of injuries sustained by women are much greater. Statistics Canada reports that in recent years, 60% of women and 25% of men sustained injuries from IPV requiring medical attention. When incidence rates of IPV and charges for criminal violence are examined, it appears that men not only perpetrate violence at higher rates but more severely.

The distinction . . . is between violence that is contained within the family, and violence where the perpetrator has a criminal history and is violent in other contexts.

There are three areas where women are decidedly more victimised but which are not focused on in studies as much as physical injuries. These areas are fear and intimidation, sexual abuse and homicide.

1. *Fear and intimidation*: [K.] Malloy et al. report on a number of studies that found that women reported significant, long term levels of fear and more negative impacts on their physical and psychological functioning, compared to male victims of female violence. [P.] Tjaden and [N.] Thoennes report that men are much more likely to make serious threats that induce significant fear in women.

2. *Sexual abuse*: Many studies have failed to include sexual abuse, which was found to be perpetrated by men up to 20 times more than for women.

3. *Homicide*: There is also a compelling difference in homicide rates, with 70% women victims killed by male partners, and 30% of men killed by female partners as reported by [D.] Saunders [in 2002]. In recent years, men are committing more homicides, and the rates for women have declined.

Style of Violence

A number of studies have attempted to 'drill down' further in order to understand gender differences in the style of violence. As previously mentioned, differences arise in research partly because samples from the criminal justice system or 'clinical' settings are compared to samples obtained from the general community. Variability between genders in the style of violence emerges when comparisons are made between community and clinical samples. Differences in violence in each context have been termed 'intimate terrorism' and 'common couple violence.' The distinction here is between violence that is contained within the family, and violence where the perpetrator has a criminal history and is violent in other contexts. Clinical samples are more likely to show 'intimate terrorism' and community samples 'common couple violence'. The studies that use the CTS in community sampling research do not capture the most severe violence. Similar distinctions are made by Holtzworth-Munroe and Stuart in 1994 in their 'family only violence' and 'anti-social domestic violence offenders' categories. The latter are predominantly men who engage in 'severe physical, sexual, and psychological abuse against intimates' [as cited in Henning and Feder's 2004 study]. Henning and Feder argue that men who perpetrate the most severe domestic violence are much more likely to have a history of criminality, but not necessarily violence, outside of the family. They imply that where this is *not* the case, violence is less severe, is less likely to escalate and the female partner is likely to be as equally violent, i.e. common couple violence.

Other studies report different styles of violence within the population of violent men. [J.] Gottman and [N.] Jacobson distinguished the 'Pit-Bull' and the 'Cobra'. The Pit-Bull is the man whose violence is purposeful, who intends to maintain dominance and control of his partner through implementing a regime of fear, using intimidation, punishment and a range of violent behaviours, including rape, stalking, beatings and threats to kill. He may or may not be violent in other contexts, but is generally intimidating and emotionally distant.

The Cobra's violence is different. He explodes if he does not get his own way. His violence is sudden and unexpected, erupting often in the context of his partner's verbal and/or physical attack. He aims to silence his partner, as well as to punish her for 'getting in his face' or for attempting to influence his life. His message is 'get away from me'. While his violence is extremely severe, he is often easier to leave.

Men have the option, more than women, to use their physical strength in response to someone else's first strike.

[K.] James et al. also found similar differences in men's violence, as reported by men to interviewers in a qualitative study examining men's construction of their own violence. They identified 'tyrants' and 'exploders'. Tyrants were similar to the 'Pit-Bulls', exercising a regime of control and terror. They most feared losing their partners, felt insecure, and were more inclined to stalk them. Exploders, on the other hand, were like the Cobras, exploding into violence when they felt provoked or attacked.

How might these differences between men who use IPV shed light on the broader gender question of who is the most serious perpetrator of IPV? Firstly, the most severe [Pit-Bulls and tyrants], and men with criminal justice histories, are capable of implementing a reign of terror backed by the threat and actuality of physical violence. They are capable of intimidating and controlling to a degree the majority of women are unable to match. Such men use violence to get their own way, have done so for a long time and will not tolerate a partner's assertion or attempts to leave. It is hard to imagine a relationship where a woman is able to instil the same fear and terror in a man through the use of such tactics.

'Exploders' described their own violence as occurring in relation to a woman's provocation or attack. If a woman attacked an exploder, he would be likely to escalate his violence, to explode in a rage perhaps aiming to gain control, to prevent injury to himself, to immobilise or injure her, but foremost to stop her attack. An exploder would do whatever it took. In other words, men have the option, more than women, to use their physical strength in response to someone else's first strike. Because of their physical strength, acts such as 'shoving' 'pushing' 'punching' or 'hitting' will inevitably cause more damage when done by a male than a female.

Common Couple Violence

But are women equally violent in 'common couple violence?' Violence that is contained to the couple relationship, Henning and Feder argue, is more likely to involve both parties, does not escalate and is less severe. This is the image of the 'tit' for 'tat' violence, mutual shoving and pushing, maybe ending in a punch from the man. It is here that women's motivations for violence differ from those of men. They are more likely to use violence in self-defence, while smaller percentages report resorting to violence to 'get through' to their partner, to engage emotionally or in retaliating for emotional hurt. How likely is it that a man would let a woman 'win' a physical fight? No doubt there are some men who are firmly committed to non-violence, or non-violence to women, who, even if their partner did attack them, they would restrain themselves.

Using the term 'common couple violence' can be misleading, because in community surveys men have been found to cause greater injury. In other words, violence that is contained to the couples' relationship is not necessary minor in nature. Men cause greater injury when they use shoving, choking, beating up or strangling their partners, whereas women do more damage when they use a weapon. The research suggests that women use implements and other means to 'equalise' their strength. The concept of 'common couple violence' is meant to suggest minor violence, and equal participation of women as perpetrators. The danger of uncritically accepting this concept is that women rarely escalate violence, they match it; the woman is most likely acting in self-defence; and the man is likely to employ his greater strength to 'win' the contest.

In Henning and Feder's study of people arrested for IPV, women were more likely to have used a weapon in the attack, and were therefore arrested more often. There were a number of differences, however, which led them to conclude that men presented the greatest risk for recidivism and men were the gender of most concern. Although the women who were arrested had committed a more severe offence, their violence was more likely than the men's to be in self-defence and they were no more likely to cause injury. Secondly, compared to men, the women in the study were less likely to escalate the conflict, or to use threats to kill. Compared to men, the women had less access to guns. Men were more likely to have histories of severe assaults, have violated protection orders, parole or probation requirements and also have a history of non-violent offences. This leads us to consider the differences in intent and motivation for violence.

Considering Intentions and Motivations

It has been frequently argued that women's violence is often in self-defence whereas men's violence is often in order to control and dominate their partner. A number of studies have found that women who have criminal justice histories and who are violent in the couple relationship are more likely to use violence in self-defence, and suffer the greatest injury. This is especially the case for homicides committed by women, who report much higher levels of fear than for men who murder their partners. Men's motives for killing their partners are more likely to involve jealousy and control, particularly in relation to termination of a relationship.

Researchers have examined the assertion that women's violence is in self-defence by seeing who out of the couple initiated the violence. Some studies found that women initiated violence more often than men. Although in these studies the women initiated physical assault, the meaning of this cannot be determined without knowing more about the context of the violence and file history of the relationship. For instance, having initiated IPV, it doesn't mean that self-defence doesn't come into play as the partner becomes more violent.

It is not that women are "nicer" or "good."... It's that relative to men, women have less power and status in heterosexual partnerships, are less able to "win" a physical fight, or assert difference without being threatened and attacked, and are more likely to be dissatisfied with the relationship and want to leave.

When women strike first, their partners' reactions are often fierce. She may receive more severe injuries, and end up fighting back in self-defence. The contest is often uneven from the start. Therefore, initiation of aggression does not mean that self-defence is not a factor as violence escalates. Straus himself points out that initiation of violence can still be in response to perceived greater harm, when there is a long history of abuse. However, it is equally likely that men might also be acting out of self-defence, if their partner initiates aggression. However, the man is usually able to use more severe violence, even when he has not initiated a particular instance.

Violent Men Are More Dangerous than Violent Women

Despite the existence of women's violence towards men, men's violence remains the more serious violation. The conclusions of my previous paper remain: men inflict greater injury; are motivated by domination, control and punishment; and are more able to instil fear and terror in women partners who, when compared with men, are less able to escape. They are more likely to sexually assault their partners, and to kill them. Women can inflict severe injury on their male partners when they use a weapon, and are as likely as men to engage in minor forms of violence. They may initiate violence in a minor way, but are likely to end up more seriously injured.

There are of course, some situations where a man is afraid, feels unable to escape and/or is seriously injured, when he himself is not violent. However, these situations are rare in comparison to the prevalence of the alternative. Nevertheless, women's violence should not be condoned, and service providers should assess claims of women's violence, especially in the light of the greater risk to her if her partner is also violent. In addition, through an exploration of women's violence, differences in degree, risk and outcomes can be explored.

It is not that women are 'nicer' or 'good'. Women are capable of misusing power, perhaps in different ways. It's that relative to men, women have less power and status in heterosexual partnerships, are less able to 'win' a physical fight, or assert difference without being threatened and attacked, and are more likely to be dissatisfied with the relationship and want to leave. The latter, wanting to leave, puts them at great risk of men's IPV.

Battered Woman Syndrome Is a Gender Issue

Gena Rachel Hatcher

At the time this essay was written, Gena Rachel Hatcher was senior articles editor of the NYU Annual Survey of American Law *in 2002–2003. She graduated from New York University School of Law in 2003.*

After years of physical violence and psychological abuse, marked by several attempts to leave her husband that failed when he found her and forced her to return, Judy Norman shot her husband while he slept. In a violent marriage racked by beatings that had only increased in severity and frequency, culminating in the initiation of divorce proceedings, the filing of several restraining orders, and a death threat, Sherrie Lynn Allery shot her husband while he lay on the couch. At the trials of both of these women, their jurors inevitably wondered why these women didn't just leave: Why did Judy Norman remain in a violent relationship? Why did Sherry Lynn Allery not seek outside assistance before resorting to such force? Why did these women truly believe *this time* the danger was imminent, though so many times before they had not left, and had not acted, and yet had survived?

Reconsidering Self-Defense

On first inspection by judges and juries alike, the traditional self-defense doctrine seems not to apply. A traditional understanding of the elements of self-defense do not fit with a battered woman's experience in which imminence, reasonableness, proportionality, and attempts to retreat are much less apparent and much more case-specific. An ordinary juror may not grasp the aggressive nature of the particular incident under review without understanding its underlying pattern of violence. For example, a battered woman may kill her spouse at a time when he is not actually physically attacking her, even in his sleep. In addition, because women are often smaller than men, she may have to use more force than a man might use in order to repel her batterer. A battered woman may not attempt to escape because she has tried before and he has found her, or because she knows that if she attempts to escape she or her children will almost certainly be killed.

Thus, in the 1970s, feminist theorists argued that the subordination of women and sexist presumptions were leading to inequalities and misconceptions in the responses of judges and juries to the self-defense pleas of battered women who killed. Expert testimony was offered at trials to explain and defend women who had killed their batterers using the "rubric of battered woman syndrome." The term served as shorthand for the growing body of scientific and clinical literature that described a condition similar to post-traumatic stress disorder. The purpose of such testimony was to aid judge and jury in evaluating the self-defense claim of the battered woman. The testimony offered explanations to the questions posed above and illuminated why a battered woman behaving reasonably might behave differently than an unbattered man or woman, or even a battered man. In addition, the testimony highlighted why a battered woman's perception of imminence was at odds with a layperson's definition of the term. It also explained why a battered woman might respond with force that might seem excessive to a juror, yet was in fact proportional to the threat. Finally, it explained why a battered woman loses faith in the possibility of retreat.

More recently, courts and state legislatures have adjusted the scope of this expert testimony to focus on "Battering and Its Effects"—a gender-neutral standard that focuses on the psychological impact that battering patterns may have on a battered person. The testimony is admissible to indicate that a defendant had the requisite state of mind to sustain a claim of self-defense despite the fact that, from a traditional self-defense perspective, the threat of harm was not "imminent" at the time of the homicide. This expert testimony has been utilized in claims of self-defense by men, as well as by women. . . .

The Foundations of the Battered Woman Syndrome

To understand why expansion of the Battered Woman Syndrome into Battering and Its Effects erodes and weakens its ability to answer our original questions, we must first return to the origins of the Battered Woman Syndrome. As discussed above, admission of expert testimony on the Battered Woman Syndrome became an accepted practice to aid juries in understanding the self-defense pleas of battered women who killed their spouses. The use of such expert testimony grew out of a need for courts and juries to understand how a battered woman's perception of imminence may have been reasonable, given her particular set of experiences. Courts used a strict and objective understanding of imminence. One court [in the 1989 North Carolina case *State v. Norman*] refused to offer jury instructions on self-defense for a battered woman who had killed her spouse, reasoning that:

> [U]nder our law of self-defense, a defendant's subjective belief or what might be 'inevitable' at some indefinite point in the future does not equate to what she believes to be 'imminent' . . . testimony about such indefinite fears concerning what her sleeping husband might do at some time in the future did not tend to establish a fear—reasonable or otherwise—of *imminent death or great bodily harm* at the time of killing.

Another court [in the 1988 Kansas case *State v. Stewart*] reversed a lower court decision to include the Battered Woman

Syndrome in its self-defense instruction to the jury, reasoning that the "self-defense instruction improperly allowed the jury to determine the reasonableness of defendant's belief that she was in imminent danger from her individual subjective viewpoint rather than the viewpoint of a reasonable person in her circumstances" and determining that notwithstanding the testimony on the Battered Woman Syndrome, the defendant was not in imminent danger close to the time of killing.

Leaving their home and their abusers may not be a real option for women who have attempted to do so in the past and failed, or whose batterers have threatened to find and injure them regardless of the outside assistance they may secure.

The foundation of the Battered Woman Syndrome included more than just the effects of the battering itself, but extended further into the defendant's mind-state to consider other experiences that contributed to the defendant's feelings of powerlessness. Most importantly, it incorporated the defendant's experiences as a woman and was intended to combat inequalities for women before the law as well as in society. Dr. Lenore Walker introduced the Battered Woman Syndrome in the psychological realm and in the legal arena, using "trauma theory together with the psychological understanding of feminist psychology, oppression, powerlessness, and intermittent reinforcement theories such as learned helplessness ... to understand the psychological impact of physical, sexual, and serious psychological abuse of the battered woman." Walker realized the need for recognition of the Syndrome in order to combat the fact that studies indicated that certain aggressive actions when perpetrated by women would be traditionally viewed as abnormal, whereas they might be viewed as understandable when committed by men. An ordinary jury would therefore be less likely to understand how a female defendant had acted reasonably in killing her batterer.

Scholars noted that an alternative to advocating admissibility of expert testimony on the Battered Woman's Syndrome would be for a female defendant to plead insanity; however, this practice would only enforce stereotypes about battered women and women more generally, in addition to being an inadequate explanation of the behaviors of these women. One court [in the 1984 case *Washington v. Kelly*] explained in greater detail:

> Self-defense and insanity raise very different concepts. In an insanity defense, the relevant inquiry is whether the mind of the accused was so affected or diseased at the time of the crime charged that he could not tell right from wrong and perceive moral qualities of his act.... In contrast, in a self-defense claim the appropriate inquiry is whether the defendant reasonably apprehended imminent death or bodily injury.

This illustrates the importance of enfolding the Battered Woman Syndrome in the self-defense doctrine to explain how the battered woman's actions were reasonable, rather than blaming them on the affliction of "insanity."

Urging the Courts to Accept Battered Woman Syndrome

The legal application of the Battered Woman Syndrome thus emerged upon this questioning of traditional self-defense requirements because of their potential sex-bias. The traditional views of self-defense, imminence, and reasonableness, did not contemplate the realities of a battered woman's experiences because "[t]raditional self-defense doctrine envisions a confrontation between male strangers. [According to Hope Toffel, it] holds that a person is justified in killing another in self-defense if a reasonable 'man' would have acted the same way." These traditional requirements proved problematic for battered women in large part because society has for so long believed that women ought to obey their husbands, having once regarded women as property of their husbands. A woman who kills her spouse would thus be automatically considered insane or inherently *un*reasonable. Courts acknowledged that wife battering "is not a new phenomenon, having been recognized and justified since Old Testament times. It goes largely unreported, but is well documented" [as quoted in *State v. Hundley*, 1985]. In addition, men are often physically stronger than women, so women may need to use more than proportional force—indeed, they may need to use deadly force—to successfully defend themselves. Thus, battered women are often compelled to kill their abusers in their sleep, when they are unaware and less likely to respond with equally deadly force. Lastly, leaving their home and their abusers may not be a real option for women who have attempted to do so in the past and failed, or whose batterers have threatened to find and injure them regardless of the outside assistance they may secure.

At one time a wife killing her husband was regarded as a much more heinous crime than if he killed her, because in "throw[ing] off all subjection to the authority of her husband" she was considered to have committed treason.

Scholars linked the patterns, behaviors, and perceptions of battered women to their role as women in a society marked by male domination, coercion and violence. Scholars explained that these women were acting in the context of a moral order that put the pressures and responsibilities of family problems on women. They found that legal, social, and medical agencies were often unsupportive and even condemning. And they acknowledged that frequent financial dependence on male spouses and other socio-economic realities either made it literally impossible for women to escape, or made it impossible for them to reasonably believe they could. Dr. Walker concluded that "a sexist society facilitates, if not actually encourages, the beating of women . . . these women do not remain in the relationship because they basically like being beaten. They have difficulty leaving because of complex psychosocial reasons. Many stay because of economic, legal, and social dependence." She further suggested that a man's "superior physical strength, and society's message that a woman belongs to a man like property" may influence a woman's self perception. Feminists and proponents of the Battered Woman Syndrome thus linked the battering of women and their responses to [what Elizabeth Schneider described as] "women's subordination within society and to more general social problems of abuse of power and control." Psychologists traced the behaviors and perceptions of battered women to inherent differences between men and women and the way they are raised in society. Accordingly, courts were urged to recognize that patterns of battering could not be viewed as a series of distinct events but had to be placed in their socio-economic context, a context characterized by both gender inequalities and stereotypes.

Validating Crucial Assumptions

Accepting the legal implications of the Battered Woman Syndrome required the validation of several crucial assumptions by the courts [as described by Elizabeth Schneider in *Battered Women and Feminist Lawmaking*]: "first, that women act in self-defense under different circumstances and in different ways than men; second, that the law of self-defense incorporates sex bias; and third, that sex-based stereotypes of women generally, and battered or raped women specifically, interfere with jurors' determinations of women's claims of self-defense." Courts recognized the need for the Battered Woman Syndrome to elucidate why battered women believed that death or serious bodily injury was imminent, not only because of the immediate effects of battering but also as a result of collective experience and history:

> Wife beating is steeped in the concept of marital privacy, and the belief that wives are the personal property of the husband. In Blackstone's Commentaries the theory of coverture was advanced, making punishment for mistreatment of a wife impossible since the husband and wife were considered one. . . . [T]raditional attitudes have made legal and actual recognition of wife beating's criminal nature slow in coming. Even after it is recognized as a crime, it is difficult to obtain even-handed enforcement. *The misconceptions have affected the battered woman's perception of herself and reduced the options available to her* [as quoted in *State v. Hundley*].

Indeed, at one time a wife killing her husband was regarded as a much more heinous crime than if he killed her, because in "throw[ing] off all subjection to the authority of her husband" [as described by Elizabeth Schneider] she was considered to have committed treason. Although this legal double standard has been eradicated, the sentiment no doubt lingers, at least to some degree. This history cannot help but form a backdrop for both the experiences of women with respect to sexism and subordination and both the subconscious and conscious sentiments of jurors.

Women lead different, "gendered lives," necessarily affected by sexism and cultural and historical subordination, and therefore kill in self-defense under different circumstances and in different ways.

Thus, stereotypes about battered women in particular, and about women more generally, enhanced the argument in favor of expert testimony on the Battered Woman Syndrome to aid jurors. Early courts reasoned that it was "widely acknowledged

147

that commonly held beliefs about battered women are subject to myths that ultimately place the blame for the battering on the battered victim. For example, battered women are generally considered to be masochists who derive pleasure from being abused." Courts concluded that these myths would obscure a jury's determination of why a battered woman stayed in a battering relationship and how this decision and her following actions were reasonable; the Battered Woman Syndrome was a helpful and necessary tool to combat these misconceptions. These feelings are the result of a history of stereotyping and must be considered and understood, rather than ignored. Dr. Walker's concepts of the "cycle theory of violence," "learned helplessness," and "powerlessness," could be "used to explain why a battered woman remains in a relationship that is both psychologically and physically harmful" where a man or ordinary juror might not.

Some courts that still use the Battered Woman Syndrome (as opposed to replacing it with Battering and Its Effects) have retained these original gendered considerations. Recent decisions that have admitted testimony on the gendered Battered Woman Syndrome have explained that such "expert testimony is useful to clarify and refute common myths and misconceptions about battered women," to attack "unstated stereotypic assumptions by explaining why the defendant stayed in the relationship, why she never sought help . . . or why she feared increased violence," and can "explain that a battered woman does not quit the relationship because she continues to love her abuser and feels that she is responsible for keeping the marriage together and rearing the children . . . [and that] members of the battered woman's own families often feel she brings the abuse upon herself" [as stated in *People v. Yaklich*, 1991, and *State v. Furlough*, 1990]. Generally, these courts have acknowledged that the self-defense doctrine and its history are "derived from a male model." [According to *State v. Gartland*, 1997], [w]omen lead different, "gendered lives," necessarily affected by sexism and cultural and historical subordination, and therefore kill in self-defense under different circumstances and in different ways. . . .

What Battered Women Have Lost

It is the very need for recognition of the differences between male and female defendants (a need acknowledged by feminist theorists) that necessitates a self-defense practice consistent with the origins of the Battered Woman Syndrome. An individualized approach that relies on the gender-neutral Battering and Its Effects has not adequately fulfilled this need. In the application of Battering and Its Effects, the differences between men and women—particularly the gendered experiences of women as a result of sexism, subordination, and stereotypical juror misperceptions—have been lost. Rather than recognizing the differences between men and women, a gender-neutral approach will take women back to pre-Battered Woman Syndrome time when a battered woman defendant was forced to defend herself against a male-dominated and male-centered perception of reasonableness and imminence. There are so many characteristics and experiences that remain exclusive to women (and thus battered women): the historical and societal sexism and subordination of women leading both to biased jury perceptions and tendencies of battered women to feel more "helpless" than battered men, the typical variance in size between men and women and their ability to defend themselves without using fatal force, and the continued (though equalizing) financial imbalance between men and women. A gender-neutral approach therefore will not appropriately educate the jury vis-à-vis the reasonableness of a battered woman's response considering these characteristics. "Male jurors are [still] more likely to minimize the violence or blame the woman; women jurors are more likely to say 'I wouldn't let that happen to me'" [as quoted in *Battered Women and Feminist Lawmaking*].

Battering and Its Effects represents dilution and backsliding in our ability to understand the actions of battered women. The psychosocial elements of the Battered Woman Syndrome are not represented by Battering and Its Effects, which necessarily only encapsulates the effects of the physical battering itself because men have not experienced the same societal and historical pressures, stereotypes, assumptions, and subordination as women. While it is true that battered men develop feelings of powerlessness, the recognition of this feeling was not the sole (nor even necessarily the most important) element resulting in the acceptance of the Battered Woman Syndrome. Rather, it was the realization that sexist presumptions prevented battered women from achieving justice in their self-defense pleas.

Societal stereotypes remain, despite the strides that have been made since the original adoption of the Battered Woman Syndrome. If we ignore this fact, we doom women to judgment racked by these stereotypes. Without addressing these concerns and realities, courts have stripped battered women of a means for explaining why they, particularly, have behaved reasonably in killing their batterer. Battering and Its Effects is not identical—by definition, the historical background of battered women, and women more generally, will not inform it. If these syndromes are "shorthand" for referencing scientific and sociological research capable of justifying a battered person's actions, then battered women are being shortchanged—Battering and Its Effects strips them of the history that underpinned the logic and necessity of the Battered Woman Syndrome. Therefore, this expansion to gender-neutrality risks the return of pervasive sexism and bias to juries without the aid of expert testimony to counter such assumptions.

Women Commit as Much Domestic Violence as Men

John Hamel

John Hamel is a licensed therapist and certified batterer intervention provider who specializes in family violence assessments and treatment programs.

In December 2005, the United States Congress passed legislation reauthorizing the Violence Against Women Act (VAWA), originally enacted in 1996. As its name suggests, this legislation has funded programs that help female victims of intimate partner violence (IPV). The new version finally acknowledged that men, too, can be victims, and allows funding to be made available for this population. This was only possible, however, because of persistent lobbying by men's rights groups, over the strenuous objections of battered women's advocates. Unless this resistance can be overcome, however, there is a strong possibility that the new legislation will have only a marginal impact on future prevention and intervention efforts with men.

The resistance comes from adherents to a particularly extreme form of feminist ideology who have shaped public attitudes and intervention policy over the past three decades by disseminating what many consider misleading and false information on IPV. Thus one finds on the official website of the National Coalition Against Domestic Violence the statement that 85 percent of IPV victims are women, while the American Bar Association's Commission on Domestic Violence puts the percentage at 90–95 percent. On the VAWNET [The National Online Resource Center on Violence Against Women] website, we are told that "women use violence for a variety of reasons, but a common one is to defend themselves. Men typically use violence to control their female partners."

The not-so-subtle point . . . is not simply that different individuals may be motivated to aggress for different reasons (which is, of course, true), but that only men intend to cause harm.

Actually, men and women assault one another at approximately equal rates and do so for similar reasons. These findings are either disbelieved or ignored, and consequently domestic violence policy consists of arresting male perpetrators and mandating them to psycho-educational batterer intervention program (BIP) groups, many of which have been shown to be only marginally effective, while providing supportive services to their female victims, despite the reality that many of them are co-perpetrators in the relationship. Men are arrested for intimate partner violence at far greater rates than women, and make up the vast majority of BIP participants. Men who have merely been accused of domestic violence may find themselves denied their parental rights. Finally, out of nearly 1,800 shelters in the United States, only the Antelope Valley Oasis Shelter in Southern California and perhaps one or two others accept male residents.

The Beginning of the Domestic Violence Movement

Wife abuse has always been prosecuted in the United States under existing assault and battery statutes. Not until the 1880s did various states enact laws specific to domestic violence, but those statutes were weakly enforced. By the 1960s and 1970s, the preferred police response to domestic disputes, including those involving physical violence, was mediation. Mental health professionals often put victims in danger by not distinguishing between less serious, mutually abusive cases from those involving life-threatening attacks by a dominant, predatory partner. The battered women's movement represented a grassroots response to this state of affairs. Initially made up of victims and their supporters, the movement was soon joined by academic feminists interested in the general advancement of women's rights. Citing victim accounts of highly controlling husbands, these feminists began to define spousal abuse as a gender issue, and provided the movement with a ready-made theory both to explain the problem and to provide a blueprint for change. In this patriarchal conception, "the correct interpretation of violence between husbands and wives conceptualizes such violence as the extension of the domination and control of husbands over their wives" [as quoted in the 1979 book, *Violence Against Wives: A Case Against the Patriarchy*, by R.P. Dobash and R.E. Dobash].

Rather than rely on interviews with abused women in shelters, the team of [Murray A.] Straus, [Richard J.] Gelles and [Suzanne] Steinmetz (1979) gathered data from large representative national sample surveys, asked both the male and female respondents about their abuse, and inquired about rates of child abuse as well as interparental violence. In contrast to the sociopolitical feminist analysis, they conceptualized partner violence within the context of interpersonal conflict. The results, indicating that in intimate relationships men and women physically assault one another at approximately equal rates, were roundly criticized. Many feminists favored women's personal accounts over statistical analyses they construed as inherently male-centered, while others criticized Straus et al.'s methodology, noting, for example, the obvious limitations of a study which did not seek information about who initiated the violence, or their reasons for doing so. "A kick with an open-toed sandal," wrote [M.] Pagelow, "administered under a bridge table and an angry kick from a pointed western boot are vastly different in both the aggressor's intent to cause injury (the social meaning behind the act) and possible injury sustained." The not-so-subtle point, with references to western boots and sandals, is not simply that different individuals may be motivated to aggress for different reasons (which is, of course, true), but that only men intend to cause harm.

By the mid-1980s, given the growing battered women's movement and media interest in high-profile public policy on domestic violence, intervention means were changing rapidly. One by one, various states enacted legislation making spousal assaults a crime. In lieu of or in addition to incarceration, perpetrators were also mandated to participate in rehabilitation programs, known as batterer intervention programs. These generally followed the model set forth by the Duluth Intervention Project, based on personal accounts of abuse from shelter women and infused with patriarchal ideology, which insists that the man is entirely responsible for interpersonal violence because he is automatically presumed, by virtue of being a male in a patriarchal society, to be the dominant partner. "When women do use violence against their spouses or cohabitants," according to Dobash and Dobash, "it is primarily in self-defense or retaliation, often during an attack by their husband." Poor impulse control and personality factors are dismissed as excuses, there is no such thing as mutual abuse, and only one dynamic exists—the three-phase cycle described by Lenore Walker. According to this scenario, (1) the man experiences internal tension, the fearful woman tries to accommodate his increasingly controlling and emotionally abusive behaviors, but she is unable to prevent (2) the inevitable explosion of violence. Relieved of the tension and recognizing that his partner might leave him or alert the police, (3) the man becomes remorseful, giving her renewed hope that he will change. But the tension mounts once again, and the cycle begins anew.

Limitations of the Patriarchal Conception

Proponents of the patriarchal conception present what at first glance seems to be plausible evidence in support of their position: From early childhood males are more outwardly aggressive than females, and as adults they commit the preponderance of violent crimes. Even in the 21st century, the status of women as a whole has yet to reach parity with that of men. Men account for the great majority of elected officials, as well as the top business executives, and would therefore be presumed to have the greater share of institutionalized power. Using socioeconomic measures, [Kersti] Yilo and [Murray A.] Straus found that the most "patriarchal" states, in which men as a whole had the greatest amount of power, also reported the highest rates of male-on-female partner abuse. The 1975 National Family Violence Survey found that the number of male-dominant households (measured according to "who has the final say" in decisions regarding having children, whether a partner should go to work, etc.) exceeded the number of female-dominant households and that marital conflict was highest among the former. Similar findings have been garnered from general population samples from South Korea and Hong Kong, and college students in the United States.

Women are as victimized in same-sex relationships, where patriarchal structures should not exist, as in heterosexual ones, and violent lesbians include "feminine" as well as "butch" types.

Notwithstanding these data, support for the patriarchal conception is tenuous at best, and certainly does not warrant the gender-biased arrest and intervention policies currently in place. For example, the research previously cited by Yilo and Straus indicated that male-on-female partner assaults were also high in the least patriarchal states. The National Family Violence Surveys did find a higher proportion of male- versus female-dominated households in the mid-1970s, but the differences were, even for that era, rather negligible, with only 9.4 percent of the households male-dominant, and 7.5 percent female-dominant. The rest were either divided-role or egalitarian power arrangement. The most significant finding was the correlation between high-conflict and physical violence in both male and female-dominant relationships.

Patriarchal explanations are also contradicted by other research findings. First, most men are neither physically assaultive nor controlling. Second, women are as victimized in same-sex relationships, where patriarchal structures should not exist, as in heterosexual ones, and violent lesbians include "feminine" as well as "butch" types.

Some studies of battered women have identified conservative gender attitudes among violent husbands, while others have found no such link. In [David] Sugarman and [S.] Frankel's comprehensive review of studies on patriarchy and partner violence, significant correlations were found between pro-violent attitudes and assaults against female partners, but traditional gender role attitudes (for example, that the woman should let the man make all the decisions and not work outside the home) did not differentiate violent from non-violent men. And surprisingly, the violent men measured lower on measures of masculinity, including goal-directed and instrumental (stereotypic masculine) versus expressive (stereotypic female) behaviors.

While women may feel inhibited from displaying aggression outside the home, societal norms excuse female aggression in the home, where women seek to defend their interests as mothers and homemakers.

Feminist theorists have not yet explained how patriarchal power translates into personal power in most relationships. One might suppose that a prominent businessman who is well-connected politically in a small town would have an advantage over an uneducated wife, especially if she lacked a network of influential friends. But most men are not so well-connected. Also, the feminist focus on institutional power ignores other forms of power that are more germane in the home setting. These include (1) the personal power that comes from having a dominant personality and (2) relationship power, which can be measured by the extent to which one person is needed by his or her partner. Thus a strong-willed woman who is ready to use whatever tactics are necessary to get her way and is married to a passive man who is emotionally dependent on her will have the power in the relationship, no matter how "patriarchal" the society is in which they live. Ironically, it is partly due to the patriarchal code of chivalry that most men are reluctant to hit their female partners, even when subjected to physical abuse.

A review by [John] Archer of cross-cultural research on general aggression found, as expected, far higher rates of physical aggression and somewhat higher rates of verbal aggression by men. Measures of anger and hostility, however, revealed few differences between the genders. Females of all ages engage in indirect aggression against peers, co-workers, and others, and adolescent girls use indirect forms of aggression at significantly higher rates than boys. Studies have shown that women, when feeling justified to do so, may engage in direct aggression if they think they will remain anonymous.

While women may feel inhibited from displaying aggression outside the home, societal norms excuse female aggression in the home, where women seek to defend their interests as mothers and homemakers. The minimization of female-perpetrated abuse is perpetuated by clinicians, who rate abusive and controlling behaviors as "more abusive" when perpetrated by a man regardless of the context, and who are unable to predict at greater than chance levels violence by women released from a psychiatric emergency room.

Why the Patriarchal Theory Argument Took Hold

Scrutinized in terms of empirical findings, one detects a number of holes in the patriarchal theory argument. Why, then, did it "take hold" so quickly, and why does it continue to shape public policy on domestic violence?

Especially among academics and policy-makers, one would suspect revenge as equally plausible an explanation as any for the callous, cynical disregard gender feminists have had for the truth.

As the NFVS indicated, a great many men were victims of IPV at the start of the battered women's movement. In fact, there have always been male victims and while past law-enforcement responses to partner violence were certainly inadequate in cases of female victims, they were hardly vigorous in protecting males, who were doubly victimized by public ridicule. But, as previously noted, it was primarily women who took up the cause of helping domestic violence victims. On the other hand, because of their socially conditioned need to present a facade of strength and downplay their victimization, abused men did not spontaneously gather in comparable numbers, and although some advocates early on cautioned against the politicization of domestic violence, the movement was inevitably co-opted by what [R.] Sommers calls gender feminists, whose radical ideology could not allow for the existence of male victims.

"Angry over a history of domination," writes Linda Kelly [in a 2003 article published in the *Journal of Interpersonal Violence*], "feminists have discredited female violence in order to give women a secret way to strike back." This is not the only explanation. Many are undoubtedly "enthralled with the power that comes with having one's philosophy hold sway and the control they feel from influencing criminal justice policy.

Ironically, they often attribute these very power and control motives to abusive men" [according to D. Dutton and K. Corvo]. Frontline workers, many of whom had been previously battered themselves, may be forgiven for their ignorance and tendency to over-generalize from their personal experiences, but as Dutton and [I.] Nicholls suggest, patriarchal theory has persisted due to groupthink and the fear engendered among those who might otherwise challenge it. Especially among academics and policy-makers, one would suspect revenge as equally plausible an explanation as any for the callous, cynical disregard gender feminists have had for the truth.

During the 1980s and 1990s, a substantial increase in domestic violence research yielded a body of often flawed, sometimes illuminating findings. These served to broaden the discussion, fuel the ongoing debate over issues of methodology and the role played by women in family violence, and undermine patriarchal theories of causation.

Personality Research and Male Batterer Typologies

From extended interviews with a sample of 400 battered women in Colorado [Lenore] Walker identified a personality profile for men who batter, featuring lower socioeconomic status (SES) than their mates, chauvinistic attitudes, and a propensity toward alcohol abuse, insecurity, emotional dependence, possessiveness, and jealousy. Using the Cattell 16-Personality Factor (16PF) test and the Michigan Alcoholism Screening Test, [J.M.] Scheurger and [N.] Reigle found high levels of violence among men in BIP groups were associated with anxiety, depression, poor self-esteem, alcoholism, and social nonconformity, including poor impulse control. [J.] Browning and Dutton theorized male batterers use violence to both reduce tension and create emotional distance from their partner out of fear of emotional intimacy or losing control. Dutton and [C.] Strachan found that violent men demonstrated a greater need for power, due to low self-esteem and feelings of powerlessness, compared to non-violent men. In a later paper, Dutton wrote:

> Patriarchy does not elicit violence against women in any direct fashion. Rather, it may provide the values and attitudes that personality-disordered men can exploit to justify their abuse of women. This distinction is an important one: It explains why the majority of men remain nonviolent and how they differ in at least one essential and nontautological aspect from violent men.

Data on the personalities of violent men came primarily from victim reports, as in the Walker study, or from clinicians without the benefit of control groups. [P.] Neidig et al. attempted to correct for this shortcoming by interviewing and extensively testing 119 military men who had perpetrated at least one act of IPV in the previous year, as well as a nonviolent control group matched for demographic variables. The physically abusive men were not found to exhibit a significantly greater degree of chauvinistic attitudes or to lack empathy for their partners. The only significant difference between the groups was that the violent men recorded lower scores on the Coopersmith Self-Esteem Inventory. The authors concluded that personality and attitudinal factors are not as important as stress and marital discord in predicting violence. They speculated that the men were not batterers in the classic sense but rather "hitters" whose violence was of the "expressive" type, largely influenced by stress and relationship dynamics, as opposed to the "instrumental" violence exhibited by more controlling types of men.

[L.] Hamberger and [J.] Hastings, recognizing that men arrested for spousal abuse did not uniformly exhibit the same degree of violence or psychopathology, categorized this population according to a cluster of distinct personality characteristics. From this work and a review of the literature, [Amy] Holtzworth-Munroe and [G.] Stuart proposed a now-famous typology of male batterers consisting of (1) family-only, (2) dysphoric-borderline, and (3) generally violent antisocial types. The family-only types were regarded as the least dangerous, with low levels of psychopathology and less serious domestic violence histories. In [Neil] Jacobsen and [John] Gottman's schema, Pit Bulls represented the dysphoric-borderline types in their intense dependency needs and desire to control their partners. Akin to generally violent, antisocial men, "cobra" types exhibited less emotional dependency, but had poor impulse control (with histories of criminal activity and substance abuse) and were capable of perpetrating severe violence, including the use of weapons. Others have attempted typologies of their own, among them Dutton, whose early two-dimensional model characterized intimate abusiveness as impulsive or instrumental on one axis, and undercontrolled or overcontrolled on the other.

Research on Contextual Factors

Because the 1975 National Family Violence Survey did not inquire about rates of initiation and self-defense, findings of comparable assault rates by men and women were easily dismissed. In the 1980s and 1990s, however, a small number of studies examined the context of IPV.

Mutuality and Initiation Rates

A second National Family Violence Survey was conducted in 1985, with a sample exceeding 6,000 respondents. To eliminate the problem of male underreporting, [Murray] Straus examined the data provided by the wives and found that in 48.6 percent of assaults, both partners were violent. The husband was the sole perpetrator in 25.9 percent of the cases and the wife was the sole perpetrator 25.5 percent of the time. A survey of 200 military couples to whom the police had responded to a domestic violence call reported an 83 percent rate of mutual assaults. In a longitudinal study of 1,037 New Zealanders, most cases of partner violence among young adults were deemed to have been mutual.

Rates of mutuality only tell us that both partners were violent. They do not indicate which partner initiated the assaults or what percentage of aggressive behavior was in self-defense. In the second National Family Violence Survey, the wives reported that they initiated the violence 53.1 percent of the time, their husbands 42.3 percent of the time. Those who could not remember who started the violence accounted for the remaining 3.1 percent of cases. The National Youth Survey, drawing on data from 1,725 respondents in the Eastern United States, yielded similar results, with 61.3 percent of the men and 54.2 percent of the women reporting that the female partner had initiated the violence in their last serious argument. A dating population study of 865 students at four universities in the South by [A.] DeMaris determined that it was the female partner more often than not who initiated the physical violence. Of the women reporting violence in a representative sample of 707 adult respondents in Alberta, Canada, 67 percent identified themselves as the initiator. High rates of female-initiated violence have also been found among couples in which the man had been court-mandated to a BIP group. In the Austin, Texas, study by [Anson D.] Shupe, [William A.] Stacey, and [Lonnie] Hazlewood, the woman initiated the assault one-third of the time. In [Edward] Gondolf's multi-site study of men's BIP groups, during a treatment follow-up period, the female victims reported they initiated the violence in 40 percent of the cases.

Gender Assumptions About Domestic Violence Should Be Re-examined

Linda G. Mills

Linda G. Mills has written extensively on family violence. She is a professor of social work, public policy, and law at New York University. She founded the Hawkins Center of Law and Services for People with Disabilities and the Center on Violence and Recovery.

I first met Brenda Aris at Frontera Prison in Southern California, where she was serving a fifteen-year to life sentence for shooting her sleeping husband. Perhaps I expected to meet someone calculating and cruel. Instead, I found Brenda to be kind and docile. Even when I learned her history of abuse, I did not fully understand where she found the strength to kill.

Over the course of many years, Brenda has shared with me the details of that fateful event. Rick Aris, her husband of eleven years, had hit her that night and had threatened her life before he passed out. Brenda did not know when Rick would wake and kill her. She genuinely believed a preemptive strike while he was asleep was her only choice. Most mainstream feminists would agree: Brenda was a victim; her violence was self-defense; and she did not deserve the second-degree murder sentence she received.

While I do not believe that Brenda deserved to serve what was ultimately almost eleven years in prison, I am not sure she was simply a victim. What I do know is that she got the gun from her neighbor's apartment, sat behind her husband on the bed they shared, and shot five bullets toward his back.

Rick Aris was a rageful, abusive man. Of that I am certain. I am also certain that Brenda shot that gun, that her violence cannot be denied. This [essay] explores the nature of women's violence and asks the critical question, Are women as violent as men? It also helps us understand more clearly how and why women's violence has been given short shrift and how this approach, in turn, has prevented us from addressing the problem more appropriately.

At the very heart of mandatory policies and the mainstream feminism that supports it lies the assumption that men abuse women and should therefore be punished for their violence.

Following the implementation of mandatory interventions, the greatest increase in arrests has been of women who are charged with domestic violence crimes. Los Angeles provides a poignant example: in 1987, a total of 340 women and 4,540 men were arrested for domestic violence crimes in that city. In 1995, after mandatory arrest policies were implemented, 1,262 women and 7,513 men were arrested for domestic violence crimes. Since the implementation of aggressive arrest policies, three times as many women have been arrested for domestic violence crimes, compared with less than twice as many men.

Most mainstream feminists would argue that the problem of dual arrest, as it is sometimes called, lies with a police officer who fails to identify the primary aggressor (the man) and therefore arrests both parties to satisfy the mandate that someone be arrested when a domestic violence crime has occurred. Sexism on the part of police officers, these advocates complain, explains why women have been arrested in such large numbers. To respond to the dual-arrest problem, supporters of mandatory arrest policies have pushed for "primary aggressor" laws that more clearly assign blame to the male perpetrator. Here I ponder a different and more troubling reason for the statistics. What if some part of the reason women are being arrested is because they are involved in a dynamic of intimate abuse?

At the very heart of mandatory policies and the mainstream feminism that supports it lies the assumption that men abuse women and should therefore be punished for their violence. Many mainstream feminists consider it heretical to suggest that women's violence may be a relevant factor in thinking about intimate abuse. They believe that even suggesting that Brenda Aris is in any way responsible minimizes the violence of true batterers, the *real* bad guys like Rick Aris. These mainstream feminists worry that if we question the assumptions upon which domestic violence policy making has been built, we will begin to blame women for men's violence and set the movement back. Yet it is crucial to understand the role of women's violence in the dynamics of intimate abuse if we want to develop new theories and methods that truly address the problem. . . .

Women as Aggressors

How researchers have defined aggression has obviously shaped the results of their research. For example, researchers in New Zealand found that when they inquired into "aggression" rather than "violence," they were more likely to elicit admissions by women that they were violent. In one study, 37 percent of the women surveyed admitted that they had perpetrated physical aggression against their male partners, compared with 22 percent of men who admitted perpetrating physical aggression against their female partners. Severe physical aggression by women also measured at significant rates. Twenty-four percent of women, versus 8 percent of men, reported using such behaviors as kicking, hitting, biting, hitting with a weapon, slapping, using or threatening the use of a knife or gun, beating up, and choking or strangling. In this same study, 95 percent of the women and 86 percent of the men reported at least one act of verbal aggression against a partner.

When the research question is narrowed to encompass "physical assault" rather than "aggression," the outcome is clearly affected. For example, in a [1997] study by [John] Langley, [Judy] Martin, and [Shyamala] Nada-Raja, men were much less likely to identify women's acts of aggression as "assault," whereas women were much more likely to label men's acts of aggression as "assault." Only 2.7 percent of the men and 11.3 percent of the women reported "assaults" by their intimate partners. These findings reflect the results that most mainstream feminists rely on when describing domestic violence: men are abusers, women are victims, and everyone should see it that way.

However, the bulk of studies on abuse in intimate relationships clearly contradict this conclusion. In a startling finding from the United States, [Murray A.] Straus, [Richard] Gelles, and [Suzanne] Steinmetz reported in 1974 that husbands and wives committed nearly equal amounts of physical violence in intimate relationships. According to these findings, 12.1 percent of husbands reported that they committed violent acts against their female partners, and 11.6 percent of wives reported acts of violence against male partners. Ten years later, their results were essentially confirmed: 11.3 percent of husbands reported violence against their wives, and 12.1 percent of wives reported violence against their husbands. What is perhaps most interesting about these studies is that they reveal that men and women, in equal numbers, report being the sole victim of violence in the intimate relationship. In other words, these studies do not in any way suggest that women's violence is a reaction to men's violence. More than one hundred studies have since confirmed these and similar findings.

A study of college students affirms that violence between young men and women who are dating and not married is also equal. Other research indicates that high school girls are at least as violent as boys in dating relationships, if not more so.

Even verbal abuse by mothers can have devastating consequences for children and later for adults.

Violence in lesbian relationships also sheds light on the issue of female aggression, [Robert L.] Bowman and [Holly M.] Morgan, who studied verbal and physical abuse in homosexual and heterosexual college students, found that in same-sex relationships, lesbians reported statistically significant higher levels of violence in all instances than women in heterosexual relationships. Lockhart and colleagues found that 90 percent of the lesbians they surveyed had experienced verbal aggression over the previous twelve months, and 30 percent reported one or more incidents of physical violence. According to [Gwat-yong] Lie and [Sabrina] Gentlewarrier, more than half of the 1,099 lesbians in their study reported that they had been physically abused by a female lover or partner. These statistics suggest that lesbians, and hence women, are not immune from exerting or experiencing violence in their intimate relationships. . . .

Intimate Homicide and Child Abuse

Intimate male partners kill their female partners more often than the reverse. What is striking, however, is how infrequently intimate homicide actually occurs. In 2001 in the United States, 1,034 men killed their female intimate partners, and 295 women killed their male partners. Although men may perform the majority of sexual abuse on women and children in the family, women are more likely to be physically abusive (though the difference between the two groups is not large).

As [Barbara A.] Wauchope and [Murray A.] Straus hypothesize, the prevalence of abuse by mothers against their children might reflect their primary caretaking responsibilities. In other words, mothers commit more child abuse because they are more likely to be exposed to a home environment. Interestingly, a report by the Bureau of Justice Statistics found similar rates of murder by mothers and fathers of children under the age of five.

The view that mother's exposure to children explains why women are likely to abuse children does not in any way excuse such behavior. Even verbal abuse by mothers can have devastating consequences for children and later for adults. Psychologist Donald Dutton reports that there may be a critical link between verbal abuse inflicted by the mother on her male child and the likelihood of the boy becoming abusive once he grows up and becomes intimate with a female partner. Dutton's finding that verbal abuse by a mother may cause a man to have extreme anger responses toward his female partner only underscores the importance of recognizing all forms of abuse—physical and emotional, male and female, parent and child—in the violence dynamic.

There is strong evidence to suggest that psychological abuse can often predict physical aggression.

Mainstream feminist activists and researchers have consistently argued that women's aggression against men is irrelevant because it inflicts so much less harm than the injuries men inflict on women. These scholars argue that psychological or even physical abuse inflicted by women is irrelevant compared with other forms of violence expressed by men. . . . This rhetorical and legal strategy of dismissing emotional abuse has the effect of ignoring all women's violence. So if the political imperatives are so great, that is, to expose the injurious nature of men's violence in an attempt to protect women, why do I persist in exposing these less significant forms of women's aggression?

A Link Between Verbal and Physical Aggression

There is strong evidence to suggest that psychological abuse can often predict physical aggression. In a study of engaged and newly married couples, [Christopher M.] Murphy and [K. Daniel] O'Leary found that "psychologically coercive behavior precedes and predicts the development of physical aggression in marriage." They also report that both partners "may contribute to the escalation of conflict tactics during the early stages of the relationship." These findings are important for two reasons. They suggest that if feminists' overriding goal is to reduce incidents of violence against women, reducing psychological aggression in both partners is likely to reduce injurious physical abuse against women. They are also important for another less obvious reason. Researchers Kevin Hamberger and Theresa Potente argue that emotional abuse should count less in terms of the hierarchy of violence because it has less potential to oppress. There is evidence that in fact this is not true—some women experience emotional abuse as much more significant than physical forms of violence. If we do not recognize women's emotional aggressiveness, it is difficult to acknowledge the ways men can be emotionally abusive, too.

It is startling, in the face of the studies described here, to realize that mainstream feminists have been so successful at repressing altogether the effect of women's aggression on intimate abuse. The primary rhetorical strategy used by mainstream feminists to achieve this success has been to minimize abuse by women by labeling it as exclusively defensive—a necessary reaction to men's violence.

In fact, when [Jan E.] Stets and [Murray A.] Straus compared the violence patterns of couples, they found that the most prevalent pattern was one in which women's violence was more severe and men's violence was less significant. Among couples who were dating, 13.5 percent reported that the women had a pattern of more severe violence, and only 4.8 percent reported the male pattern to be more severe. In cohabitating couples, 1.2 percent reported that men's pattern of abuse was more severe, compared with 6.1 percent who reported that women's abuse was more severe. In married couples, 2.4 percent reported a pattern of "more" severe violence for men, compared with 7.1 percent who reported that women represented the more severe pattern.

A Distinction Between Men's and Women's Violence

Let us return to the fact that what is distinct about men's and women's violence is the degree to which women, although aggressive and violent in their own right, are more likely to be injured by men than vice versa. Stets and Straus found that 7.3 percent of the women who reported severe violence against them by men needed medical attention, compared with 1.0 percent of the men reporting severe violence. This is consistent with [Richard A.] Berk, [Sarah F.] Berk, [Donileen R.] Loseke, and [David] Rauma's study of 262 domestic disturbance calls. When ranked according to injury, 43 percent of the women were found to have been injured; 7 percent of male victims had injuries.

Since men were much more likely to injure women, and hence come within the criminal law's judgmental gaze, women's expressions of abuse, both physical and emotional, could be both minimized and ignored.

Mainstream feminist activists recognized early on the importance of this distinction to their legal advocacy efforts. Separating emotional and physical violence meant that female victims of injurious domestic violence would get legal recognition, and their complaints about the violence in their intimate lives would be addressed. Indeed, as mainstream feminism developed these judgments about the relative importance of men's violence and the insignificance of women's aggression, these attitudes became incorporated into the lexicon of the culture at large. The fact that women themselves might be physically abusive or that indirect aggression occurred at all became irrelevant. What was also lost was the idea that women in abusive relationships did not necessarily want the legal reaction mainstream feminists had tailored for them, nor did they believe that they were blameless.

Given the overwhelming evidence of women's emotional and physical abuse toward others, how have mainstream feminists maintained their conviction that these powerful findings should be ignored? How have they developed, so vehemently, the view that domestic violence is one-sided and male, and not part of a dynamic between two people?

Studies of reformed batterers suggest that although many men can stop physically abusing their partners, they are often unable to control their emotionally abusive tendencies.

Assumptions Based on Gender Stereotypes

To answer, I will offer a brief history of the deliberate effort by the battered women's movement to separate severe physical male-oriented violence that could or did result in injury from insignificant female physical or emotional abuse for the ultimate goal of criminalizing domestic abuse. This move, as I will describe it, contributed a great deal to the view that what mattered was the concrete manifestation of abuse in the form of injury. Since men were much more likely to injure women, and hence come within the criminal law's judgmental gaze, women's expressions of abuse, both physical and emotional, could be both minimized and ignored.

This minimization was consistent with gender stereotypes (a hold-over from the 1950s) that asserted the view that women were both physically weak and emotionally subservient to men and were therefore incapable of emotional, let alone physical, harm. Any aggression by women—physical or emotional—was insignificant compared with men's violence. Moreover, women's physical violence was only one of two things: if it was severe, it was defensive; if it was not severe, it was not to be taken seriously. Physical abuse by women was often seen by men as less serious, and perhaps more like a joke or, at most, an emotional outburst. For example, [Felicity A.] Goodyear-Smith and [Tannis M.] Laidlaw found that men were reluctant to characterize slaps, hits, and punches from women as "assaultive." They also found that of the 144 men who reported being the subject of violent acts by female partners, only 14 of those considered the women's acts as assaultive or "deliberately intended to harm." Because these attitudes held by men about women's aggression resonated with what the culture still largely believed, people held on to these gendered assumptions and embraced the feminist stand on domestic violence, which asserted men's exclusive role in committing it.

The Separation of Emotional and Physical Abuse

Despite strong cultural tenets that deny the importance of women's aggression, both physical and emotional, there is now little doubt that the wounds, physical *or* emotional, caused by abuse by an intimate partner can be deep and long-lasting. Indeed, some scholars have suggested that emotional abuse can have a more enduring effect on the psyche than physical abuse. We also know that emotional abuse can cause people to become physically violent; physical abuse can create an environment fraught with emotional upheaval. Studies of reformed batterers suggest that although many men can stop physically abusing their partners, they are often unable to control their emotionally abusive tendencies. Studies of women's aggression suggest that emotional abuse is one of women's most powerful weapons. If emotional abuse is such an integral part of physical violence, and even an independent threat, then why has it been completely ignored by the law?

Elizabeth Schneider, a law professor, documents the history of feminist lawmaking in the area of domestic violence and offers an explanation for why emotional abuse was never incorporated into legal reform efforts. She finds that although there was some desire by mainstream feminists to include emotional abuse in domestic violence doctrine, feminist advocates ultimately capitulated to the path of reform that was most likely to guarantee success. Emotional abuse was too broad and unwieldy for the law. By focusing on physical violence, feminists found there was real promise for achieving the legal reform they desired. Because physical violence was already a common element of existing criminal law, there was less involved in extending its reach to the intimate sphere. Emotional abuse, on the other hand, posed particular difficulty because it was not easily defined or quantified. Schneider explains that feminist activists of the 1960s strategically uncoupled physical from emotional abuse to protect judges and the larger society from "the pain involved in acknowledging that issues of power and control are troublingly characteristic of all intimate relationships."

The social construction of domestic violence, as we might think of it, was in part a reaction to the desperation women in abusive relationships and advocates felt historically as they faced the criminal justice system's indifference to their suffering. This was an urgent time. Women were being beaten by their male partners, and professionals, such as police officers and prosecutors, were completely indifferent, even hostile, to women's cries for help. To get the nation's attention, feminists had to be loud, unwavering, and wholly righteous. In an attempt to get the attention women needed to address the injuries inflicted on them by their intimate partners, feminist advocates defined such acts by their severity, by the injuries they produced, and by the men who caused these harms. Domestic violence involved violent men—batterers—and the women they injured. Whatever women did in response, physical or emotional, was irrelevant. The strategy worked. Emotional abuse, indeed, all women's aggression, was deliberately disentangled from physical abuse to achieve the instrumental purpose of legal reform.

One obvious by-product of characterizing intimate abuse as more "physical" than "emotional" is that policy makers, judges, and other professionals came to see intimate violence as exclusively male. Emotional abuse, and the physical aggression committed by women that was taken less seriously, was delegitimized. Women's most powerful contributions to the potentially abusive intimate dynamic were minimized. To further legitimize the physical/emotional, harmful/harmless, and male/female divides, scholars began to research the physical, injurious, and male manifestations of violence.

By particularizing domestic abuse as distinctly "physical," "harmful," and "male," for the purpose of obtaining legal recognition, mainstream feminists could ignore the reciprocity that so often accompanies intimate abuse. This created four distinct problems. First, rather than seeing domestic violence as a series of interactions or a dynamic that might or might not include injury and might or might not warrant the state's scrutiny and intervention, the problem was constructed as a crime between a person who causes injury and a person who falls prey to it. Second, by erasing emotional abuse from intimate abuse, women could neither legitimately complain about men's psychological violence nor take responsibility for their own emotionally aggressive impulses or reactions. Third, and correlatively, by constructing the problem of domestic violence as exclusively physical, and caused by patriarchy, men were prohibited from developing a language to talk about their own experiences of emotional or physical abuse by their female partners. Finally, by ignoring the possibility that women inflict harm, lesbian violence was rendered all but invisible. Uncoupling physical and emotional abuse, harmful from harmless, and male from female, while elevating one over the other, meant that women were essentially removed from the violent dynamic and men were held entirely accountable for it.

CHAPTER 4

Are Efforts to Reduce Family Violence Effective?

Chapter Preface

When Jessica Lenahan of Castle Rock, Colorado, separated from her abusive husband, Simon Gonzales, in May 1999, she was granted a restraining order that required him to remain at least 100 yards away from her and the couple's three daughters except during scheduled visitations. According to Lenahan, Gonzales continued to stalk and harass her even after the restraining order was made permanent in June 1999. Her calls to Castle Rock police were, however, dismissed. Two weeks later Simon Gonzales kidnapped the three girls, who were ages seven, nine, and ten. Lenahan repeatedly contacted Castle Rock police by phone and in person throughout the night to report the abduction, but their response, in her view, was inadequate. Hours later Gonzales turned up at the Castle Rock police department with a semiautomatic handgun he had purchased earlier that night and opened fire. He was killed by police. The three girls' bodies were later discovered in the back of his pickup truck.

In June 2000 Lenahan—whose name at the time was still Jessica Gonzales—sued the Castle Rock police department for failing to protect her and her children. Although the Colorado District Court dismissed the case, the Tenth Circuit Court of Appeals reversed the decision in October 2002, and in April 2004 the Tenth Circuit Court ruled that Lenahan had the right to police protection based on the terms of her restraining order. The city of Castle Rock appealed that decision, and in November 2004 the U.S. Supreme Court agreed to hear the case. The following year, in June 2005, the Supreme Court ruled against Lenahan, arguing that a restraining order does not guarantee a constitutional right to police protection.

Frustrated and distraught, Lenahan took an unusual step for a domestic violence victim: She allowed the American Civil Liberties Union (ACLU) to petition the Inter-American

Commission on Human Rights (IACHR) in Washington, D.C.—an international human rights tribunal—to hear her case. Six months later the ACLU filed a report with the United Nations Human Rights Committee (UNHRC) as part of a review of U.S. compliance with the International Covenant on Civil and Political Rights. In July 2006 Lenahan accompanied ACLU representatives to a convention of the UNHRC in Geneva, Switzerland, where she presented her story to the United Nations' Special Rapporteur on Violence against Women.

In a historic decision, the IACHR agreed in October 2007 to hear Lenahan's case. According to the ACLU, Lenahan's case represents the first time an individual victim of domestic violence has brought suit against the United States for violating the international code of human rights. In addition to seeking redress for the violation of her and her daughters' human rights, Lenahan and her attorneys hope the case will lead to changes in the way courts and police deal with domestic violence cases as well as an official pronouncement from the IACHR on the U.S. obligation to uphold international human rights standards for domestic violence victims.

In her statement before the United Nations in Geneva, Lenahan said, "I want to make sure that no parent, anywhere, ever has to go through the pain that I went through. I want to make sure that police are ultimately accountable for doing their jobs. A restraining order is the only legal alternative offered for protection against domestic violence. If the police will take no action to enforce an order of protection then we need to know this before we go through the process and make our stalker or abuser even angrier, and maybe even incite them to murder."

Even after the passage of the 1994 Violence Against Women Act (VAWA)—which laid out fairly clear standards for law enforcement and courts to deal with family violence—prevention programs have been mired in controversy. In fact, many argue that VAWA's stipulations have made things worse rather than better. Court-ordered batterer intervention classes have failed to produce measurable results in most cases; by and large, they do not appear to change abusers' attitudes about their actions or their victims, and there is a high rate of recidivism (batterers returning to their criminal behaviors) among participants. In addition, mandatory arrest policies can be misapplied by police inadequately trained in family violence intervention. And removing children from their biological parents sometimes causes more harm than good. Many experts believe that the most successful programs are those that take a holistic approach to the problem, engaging the entire community in developing action plans. Nonetheless, many victims do not receive the help they need, and they feel isolated and ignored. In response, some have sought justice in civil, rather than criminal, courts, suing their batterers for monetary compensation. The following chapter explores the various methods groups have taken to stem family violence, examining what works, what does not work, and where there is hope for change.

Community-Based Efforts to Reduce Family Violence Work

Stacy Teicher Khadaroo

Stacy Teicher Khadaroo is a staff writer for The Christian Science Monitor.

Under the thumb of an abusive husband, it's not easy to take college courses. Susan tried. But when she sat down to study, her husband would complain that she wasn't making supper. He controlled access to their car, their cellphone, their money.

A friend who had been through it herself recognized patterns of abuse and urged Susan to seek help. With support from a community center for domestic violence survivors, she moved out last year with her son and daughter. Within a month, the center had helped her enroll at the Chelsea, Mass., campus of Bunker Hill Community College. Through a groundbreaking partnership between the college and Harbor-COV (Communities Overcoming Violence), Susan received a grant covering tuition for one course, child care, and books. And she instantly joined a supportive network of counselors and fellow students breaking free from abusive relationships. (She agreed to tell her story on the condition that her real name be withheld.)

The Need for Education

The need for additional education "is one of the significant common issues for survivors [of abuse]," says Rita Smith, executive director of the National Coalition Against Domestic Violence. Often they have to master new skills to earn higher incomes and support children without a partner; they may be immigrants with college degrees but not enough English skills to obtain credentials in the United States; or their attempts to further their education may have been sabotaged. The partnership—the Chelsea Community Education and Support Initiative—also signifies a renewed effort at many community colleges to boost retention rates by offering students more support. Help in coping with nonacademic responsibilities such as work and family is one area identified as needing improvement by the Community College Survey of Student Engagement, conducted annually by the University of Texas, Austin. In 2006, 24 percent of students said their college did well in this area, while 43 percent said their college did very little.

Reducing Obstacles

Ms. Smith hopes to see more such partnerships emerge. "It can reduce a huge number of obstacles," she says. "The more resources we can bring in from the community, the more likely it is that [survivors] are going to be able to end the violence."

With a smile of quiet pride, she describes how her kids sit at a small red table next to her computer so they can all do homework together.

For Susan, moving out on her own was a huge relief—"just knowing that [my ex-husband] had no control over whether or not I got an education. . . . Being able to sit down and do [homework] without anybody bothering me, it was good." To be a teacher at a day-care center, an associate's degree will eventually be a job requirement, and she'd like to get even more schooling so she can run her own center someday.

She pulls out a folder of homework that's covered with loving messages from her 8-year-old daughter. With a smile of quiet pride, she describes how her kids sit at a small red table next to her computer so they can all do homework together. "I like them seeing that I have good study habits."

HarborCOV helps 300 people a year with emergency shelter, but about 3,000 people from the immigrant-rich community near Boston seek counseling, transitional housing, child care, and other services in the wake of domestic violence.

In a survey two years ago, 35 percent said they wanted to continue their education, but they needed financial and other types of assistance, says Analia Lemmo, HarborCOV's economic development coordinator. Child care for evening courses is difficult to find, and financial aid often doesn't cover classes for English as a second language, she says. "The other barrier has to do with self-esteem. . . . People that have gone through domestic violence and abuse, they usually have doubts about their own capacity. . . . They need to sometimes have reassurance that they can do this."

The organizers received a $20,000 grant from the Boston Foundation to launch the initiative in the fall of 2006. Nearly 20 people signed up to attend a class of their choice and meet regularly with advisers and the group. At the end of the school year, 87 percent were still enrolled—a retention rate that organizers found surprisingly high. This year, with a $25,000 grant from the Stratford Foundation Inc. in Needham, Mass., they expect about 25 students to participate, including some who started last year.

We think this project has potential to be replicated in other communities.

"The goal is to give them everything they need so they can overcome the barriers they're facing, but we also want to treat them just like every other college student," says Judith Graham, a staff member at Bunker Hill who oversees the grant.

Advisers help students apply for financial aid and find other resources so they can continue their studies beyond what the grant covers.

Confidence Soars

Ms. Lemmo has seen the confidence of participants soar. Whether they have mastered computer skills that improved their performance on the job or have begun degree programs that they couldn't have imagined before, they take great pride in their accomplishments, she says. "Chelsea is a small community. . . . Sometimes you're walking and someone comes up and says, 'Look at my grade. . . . I got an A!'" At the end of the academic year, she surveyed participants and all of them wanted to get into a degree program, if they weren't already. "We think this project has potential to be replicated in other communities," Lemmo says. She hopes this year they'll be able to offer technical service to other Massachusetts community colleges and domestic-violence organizations that want to pair up.

Ms. Miller meets with them and calls to check in, especially when midterms or finals are approaching. "We're working hard to keep them engaged," she says. But she's seen Susan and some others become very independent: "I was delighted when [Susan] came in at the beginning of this academic year to let me know that she had, on her own, solved a tricky scheduling problem."

Susan, a high school graduate, took one course at a time last year, but she gained enough confidence to take on two courses this semester—college-level English and algebra. Still working 30 hours a week, she sometimes fits in homework while she's cooking dinner. The monthly meetings with other students from HarborCOV help keep her going. "This one woman last year . . . she had her baby and she was back in class the next week," she says. "I was like, 'That's incredible! If she can do it, you definitely can do it.'"

Coordinating Social Service Agencies Provides Comprehensive Anti-Violence Programs

The Harvard Project on American Indian Economic Development

Founded by professors Stephen Cornell and Joseph P. Kalt at Harvard University in 1987, the Harvard Project on American Indian Economic Development is housed within the Malcolm Wiener Center for Social Policy at the John F. Kennedy School of Government, Harvard University.

Responding to the alarming frequency of domestic abuse and sexual assault among the Mississippi Band of Choctaw Indians, the Tribe's Department of Family and Community Services created the Family Violence and Victim's Services Program (FVVS) in 1999. By coordinating various agencies—including Choctaw Law & Order, Choctaw Social Services, Choctaw Behavioral Health, and the US Attorney's Office—FVVS ensures that victims receive comprehensive care and that perpetrators are dealt with appropriately. Just as essential as promoting the overall physical and emotional health of the Tribe, FVVS is changing the citizens' attitude about an important topic that often remains unaddressed.

Although the Mississippi Band of Choctaw Indians' 30-year economic renaissance is widely cited as being one of Indian Country's greatest success stories, several aspects of the Tribe's social health have been slow to improve. In the late 1990s the Tribe commissioned a Mississippi State University study which found that a surprisingly high number of Choctaw homes experienced serious social problems including poor marital relations, verbal and physical aggression, sexual abuse, substance abuse, mental illness, and the intergenerational transmission of trauma resulting from cultural genocide. All of these problems contributed to a disturbing pattern of domestic violence.

Domestic violence was rising to epidemic levels among the Mississippi Choctaw. It was also one of the most underreported crimes. Many Choctaw offenders considered domestic violence to be an "internal family matter" rather than a criminal offense. Sadly, violence in the household is frequently tolerated and a pervasive attitude exists that there is nothing unusual or wrong about abusing family members. Not surprisingly, victims often remain silent. They may fear a stigma for attempting to end violent relationships or for carrying family matters into the courts. Victims also might feel that domestic abuse is not their problem, but the perpetrator's. Or, they become convinced that violence is an acceptable method of marital and familial interaction. As one Choctaw woman learned from her mother-in-law: "Your husband only does this to you because he loves you and wants you to stay."

Such learned attitudes which, it should be noted, are typical in Native and non-Native communities everywhere, allow domestic violence to quietly fester. Unfortunately, the intergenerational toll of domestic violence is high; research finds that children who grow up in homes wracked by violence are more likely to become victims or perpetrators of violence in their own homes.

In 1999, the Mississippi Band of Choctaw Indians' tribal government decided that something had to be done to abate domestic violence. It decided to launch a domestic violence prevention program that would protect victims, monitor and reeducate perpetrators, and break the cycle of silence. Thus, the Family Violence and Victim's Services Program (FVVS) was born. Administered under the Band's Department of Family and Community Services, the Program brings together the financial, human, and technical resources of five different grant projects. It is staffed by a program director (who is also an attorney), a legal secretary, a victim assistance coordinator, a women's advocate, a victim assistance therapist, and a family violence counselor.

The Program works through several complementary strategies to combat domestic violence and its aftermath. Drawing upon the legal expertise of the staff, FVVS drafts and helps enforce laws that can help stem family violence. In 2000, for example, it drafted a Choctaw domestic violence code that was subsequently enacted by the Tribal Council. Since then, FVVS has consistently worked to expand the code's reach and effectiveness in combating domestic violence; in both 2002 and 2003, it augmented and revised the code. Based upon these successes, FVVS is part of a committee that is now drafting a complementary code that will protect the rights of vulnerable adults, particularly the elderly and infirm.

FVVS staff works to offer victims of domestic violence the kind of support and protection that was once lacking. For example, FVVS initiates one-on-one contact with all victims of domestic violence or sexual assault who are either identified in police reports or approach the Program for services. It offers legal representation for those victims who seek protection orders against their abusers. The Program provides victims assistance in identifying alternate housing, finding employment, accessing transportation to court or to a shelter, and receiving translation during court proceedings. Counseling and therapy are offered to both victims and perpetrators, serving the latter largely through a court-mandated Batterer's Reeducation Program which it supervises.

While tailored to the needs of the Choctaw community, FVVS offers more services than most programs in the state of Mississippi. This is the result, in part, of FVVS's extensive coordination with relevant agencies, including the Choctaw Social Services, Choctaw Health Center, Choctaw Behavioral Health, Choctaw Law and Order, and the Choctaw Attorney General's Office. This collaboration ensures that FVVS readily addresses victims' physical, emotional, and legal needs under a single roof. Regular meetings of representatives allow for a review of each month's challenges and successes in order to continue to enhance victims' services. Interagency cooperation also provides necessary cross-discipline expertise. For example, Choctaw Health Center nurses now possess excellent equipment for documenting abuse and are trained to take photos that meet court standards. Such collaboration reduces frictions among agencies, allowing all professionals to focus on victims' needs. This is especially critical to Choctaw victims who may request services from any one of the Tribe's seven communities within ten counties.

The Program also works to raise community awareness. For instance, FVVS established resource centers, in partner facilities, that provide information about its services and educational booklets on topics such as domestic violence, rape, sexual assault, and elder abuse. Further awareness is cultivated through an in-house resource center that consists of educational booklets, videos, and children's games dealing with family violence and anger. Every October FVVS marks Domestic Violence Awareness Month by sponsoring events and hanging "Stop Domestic Violence" banners in each Choctaw community. The Program routinely publishes articles in the Choctaw Community News and disseminates flyers, posters, brochures, and promotional items.

FVVS's commitment to drafting strict domestic violence codes, supporting victims through effective interagency collaboration, and raising public awareness has produced remarkable successes. Most notably, the Tribe has realized a significant increase in the identification and reporting of domestic violence crimes. In 1998 and 1999, Choctaw Law and Order received 542 calls reporting domestic violence. In

2000, 2001, and 2002, however, following the establishment of FVVS, it received 1,111 calls. These calls resulted in 457 arrests for domestic violence crimes and over 682 FVVS follow-up contacts with domestic violence victims. FVVS obtained more than 250 court orders for clients seeking protection from their abusers and graduated more than 200 perpetrators from their Batterer's Reeducation Program.

Behind the numbers, Family Violence and Victim's Services positively changes people's lives. For example, one Batterer's Reeducation Program participant reflected that he never realized he was part of the cycle of continued violence. He truly thought that domestic violence was a part of life. However, with the assistance of FVVS, he now understands why domestic violence is not acceptable and sees how he can change his behaviors.

These numbers and similar rehabilitation stories offer compelling evidence that FVVS is succeeding in changing Choctaw perceptions of domestic violence. FVVS is shifting Choctaw citizens' tendency to willfully ignore or dismiss incidents of domestic violence. Now, tribal citizens discuss and report its occurrence more openly. While domestic violence was once a private family matter, it is increasingly viewed as a serious public health issue that affects the entire tribal community. FVVS is moving rapidly toward the realization of one of its long-term goals: that every Choctaw citizen embraces a zero-tolerance attitude with respect to domestic violence. Not only the collaborating agencies, but also the tribal government offers its support of this agenda. With this vital support, the Program's activities and actions command respect.

These accomplishments are the result of four strategic decisions that can inform other Indian nations' efforts to develop their own violence prevention programs. First, FVVS is the result of an impressive coordination of tribal revenue and five funding sources, ranging from the US Department of Justice's STOP Violence Against indian Women grant program to the state of Mississippi's Department of Public Safety, which administers a fund through the State's Victims of Crime Act. While seeking and maintaining financing for a multi-function violence prevention program is challenging, it generates distinct advantages for Choctaw citizens. Rather than seeking services from separate organizations, they can access a variety of victim-oriented services from a single operation. And FVVS is better able to synchronize its services, which helps it most effectively promote the safety, health, and autonomy of domestic violence victims and their families.

Second, FVVS replicates this focus on coordination in its interagency partnerships that are vital for serving victims' interests and to the overall success of the Program. For example, FVVS is an active member of the Protocol Committee charged with the task of developing the procedures that guide interagency coordination. The Committee's monthly meetings refine the effectiveness of sharing information, strengthening communication, increasing efficiency, and providing maximum protection for domestic violence victims. Through such procedures and protocols, and through less formal outreach, FVVS is able to work in conjunction with Choctaw law enforcement agencies, health services, and the judiciary. These forms of inter-agency familiarity and reliance make law enforcement and case management more efficient and comprehensive, and enhance their abilities to tailor services to individual victims and offenders. For instance, Choctaw Law and Order alerts FVVS of the arrest of an offender who has repeatedly been released on bail, FVVS may contact the tribal attorney general who may, in turn, alert the judge to the offender's criminal history and request that bail be denied.

Third, FVVS has undertaken important government-building work in drafting and enacting the Choctaw domestic violence code. Through its grounding in Choctaw culture, the code is both enforceable and effective. It clearly states that "violence against family members is not in keeping with Choctaw values that hold the family sacred." Accordingly, the code contains strict guidelines for the treatment of domestic violence crimes including mandatory arrest, a twenty-four hour holding period, and a mandatory twenty-six week Batterer's Reeducation Program for offenders, a firearms prohibition and enhanced sentencing for repeat offenders, and a no-drop policy for the prosecution. Initially mirroring federal law, these guidelines now acknowledge Choctaw cultural realities. For example, the firearms prohibition modification takes tribal hunting needs into account, and the reeducation program eliminated negative reinforcement already influencing offenders in their daily lives. Notably, the code also formalizes the roles of FVVS' partners, and complements and enhances the partnerships noted above. Rightly, the Choctaw domestic violence code has become a model for other tribes to learn from.

Fourth, FVVS strengthens the self-determination of the Mississippi Choctaw by strengthening its individual citizens. By assisting individuals and families to overcome a problem that is connected to other debilitating social problems, the Tribe is addressing a national crisis. The Program offers holistic and accessible services that foster a sense of empowerment in former victims, enabling them to make better choices for themselves and their families. FVVS's Batterer's Reeducation Program encourages offenders to evaluate and learn from their behaviors. As one offender contemplated his life before the Program, he remarked: "I suppose either I or someone else would be dead." FVVS literally helps the Mississippi Band of Choctaw to build human capital through healing and also prevents victimization and/or loss of tribal citizens.

An Indian nation's human capital deserves such an investment. In changing community attitudes toward domestic violence, FVVS enhances its own citizens' respect for their own and other individuals' worth. The community-wide zero-tolerance attitude FVVS is striving for will undoubtedly result in further decreases in domestic violence crimes, and in turn, increase the health and productivity of the Mississippi Band of Choctaw Indian's most precious resource: its own people.

The successful enforcement of tribal domestic violence laws requires coordination between key law enforcement, justice, and social service personnel, and close attention to the cultural considerations that may impact the laws' effectivenes.

There is no substitute for effective and efficient program administration; as demonstrated by Family Violence and Victim's Services, solid program administration is critical to creating a consistent funding stream, inter-agency partnerships, and providing first-rate client services.

Programs that promote individual and family healing make the whole nation stronger; they build human capital that, ultimately, supports tribal well-being and self-governance.

The Federal Violence Against Women Act (VAWA) Has Damaged Efforts to Reduce Family Violence

Respecting Accuracy in Domestic Abuse Reporting (RADAR)

Respecting Accuracy in Domestic Abuse Reporting is a nonprofit and nonpartisan organization that advocates for improvements in domestic violence programs and laws.

The Violence Against Women Act was enacted in 1994 by President Bill Clinton to prevent and treat intimate partner abuse. Since that time, many abused women have received sorely needed services and public awareness of the problem has been raised.

But has VAWA reduced the overall level of partner abuse? Have VAWA programs paid heed to the needs and wishes of abused women? Have they respected and supported the families and communities in which women live? Have VAWA programs balanced the needs of victims with the due process rights of alleged offenders?

In short, has the Violence Against Women Act delivered on its promises to women?

To answer those questions, we first need to understand the dynamics of partner aggression. Nearly 200 scholarly studies of domestic violence reveal that:

- Women are at least as likely as men to engage in partner violence.

- In about half of all cases, the aggression is mutual and there is no clear-cut initiator.

- About two-thirds of those cases are *minor* (e.g., shoving, throwing a pillow), while the remaining one-third involve *severe* incidents (e.g., hitting with a fist or attacking with a weapon).

The Violence Against Women Act provides funding to develop counseling, medical, and offer services for victims of domestic violence; to step up law enforcement programs to prevent partner assault; and to aggressively prosecute perpetrators. As a result, 1,500 domestic violence laws have been passed at the state level that overhauled the legal framework for addressing partner abuse. These laws:

- Provide for a broad range of benefits to domestic violence victims.

- Mandate treatment programs for abuse perpetrators.

- Allow for the easy availability of domestic restraining orders.

- Encourage or mandate arrest.

- Encourage jurisdictions to adopt "no-drop" prosecution policies.

But many of these laws are based on questionable assumptions and may infringe on civil liberties. A sizeable number of VAWA-funded services lack evidence of effectiveness. Indeed, VAWA programs have been criticized for ignoring a large segment of the domestic violence problem. . . .

No Proof that VAWA Has Reduced Intimate Partner Abuse

Violent crime of all types—robberies, simple assaults, and aggravated assaults—has been falling in the United States for many years. That long-term decline also has been observed for intimate partner crimes.

In 1976, 2,944 men and women were victims of intimate partner homicide. By 1994, the year that VAWA was enacted into law, that number had fallen to 2,087 persons—a 29% drop. So fatal partner crime began to fall long before VAWA had been passed.

An examination of *non-fatal* victimization points to a similar conclusion. Since VAWA targets aggression by intimate partners, one would expect victimization rates for that type of abuse to drop more than violence perpetrated by a stranger or friend/acquaintance. But Department of Justice statistics for the period 1995 to 2004 show that victimization of women fell across the board, regardless of who perpetrated the crime. . . .

Over the 10-year period [from 1995 to 2004], violent crime against women fell at almost identical rates, regardless of the offender category:

- Stranger—52%

- Intimate partner—55%

- Friend or acquaintance—63%

Hence, there is no evidence that VAWA-funded programs have accelerated the drop in intimate partner homicides or non-fatal crimes.

Aggressive Prosecution Policies Place Women at Greater Risk

Three studies reveal that get-tough prosecution measures may actually make things worse for female victims of partner aggression:

Mandatory Arrest for Restraining Order Violations: Many states have enacted laws that mandate arrest and prosecution in the event of a restraining order violation. One Department of Justice-funded project studied the effectiveness of such prosecution policies and concluded, "Increases in the willingness of prosecutors' offices to take cases of protection order violation were associated with *increases in the homicide* of white married intimates, black unmarried intimates, and white unmarried females." (emphasis added)

Mandatory Arrest for Assault: Another analysis of arrest policies found that women whose partners were arrested under mandatory arrest laws were far less likely to request police assistance in the event of future of violence. This is worrisome because if persons don't report the abuse, the criminal justice system is of only marginal relevance to persons who need help.

No-drop Prosecution: Sixty-six percent of prosecutors' offices have implemented so-called "no-drop" prosecution, in which the prosecutor continues the case despite the victim's stated wishes to the contrary. But one National Institute of Justice analysis warns, "We do not know whether no-drop increases victim safety or places the victims in greater jeopardy."

Real Victims Have to Compete with Minor Cases to Get Help

Our nation's broadly defined domestic abuse laws have opened the flood gates to minor allegations of domestic "violence." Currently, half of all restraining orders do not include even an *allegation* of physical abuse. Elaine Epstein, former president of the Massachusetts Bar Association, once revealed, "Everyone knows that restraining orders and orders to vacate are granted to virtually all who apply . . . In many cases, allegations of abuse are now used for tactical advantage."

A case involving a well-known media personality illustrates the problem:

> New Mexico Judge Daniel Sanchez issued a restraining order to protect Colleen Nestler. According to Nestler, a man had been sending her mental telepathic messages over the past 11 years expressing his desire to marry her. Her alleged harasser: CBS talk show host David Letterman.

One commentator [W. McElroy] deplored the questionable basis of the Letterman case, arguing that the "abuse of temporary restraining orders endangers real victims."

Likewise, one National Institute of Justice report questioned the wisdom of mandatory arrest laws, saying that "arrests for all suspects may unnecessarily take a community's resources away from identifying and responding to the worst offenders and victims most at risk."

In short, court dockets have become choked with minor and even vindictive complaints of abuse. As a result, the voices of the real victims of violence often go unheard.

> Judge Rucker Smith, of Sumter County, Georgia, was assaulted by his ex-girlfriend. Even though she had instigated the incident and he did not retaliate, he was charged with battery. A jury later acquitted Smith of all charges. The judge subsequently recounted, "For someone to fairly accuse another out of anger and vengeance silences the voices of the many real victims." [Z. Hudson]

No-Drop Prosecution Ignores Women's Wishes

The majority of abuse cases involve disputes in which the conflict is a minor, mutual, and/or one-time occurrence. Women often believe these situations can be handled better through counseling rather than legal intervention. So in about 80% of cases, women who request police assistance later recant or decide to drop the charges.

As discussed above, "no-drop" prosecution policies often discourage women from seeking police help in the event of future violence. No-drop is controversial for other reasons, as well. If the woman refuses to testify, the prosecutor may charge her with obstruction of justice and threaten to take away her children. In one case, the county prosecutor put a woman in jail for 8 days after she refused to testify against her boyfriend. She later won a $125,000 settlement for false imprisonment.

New York University professor Linda Mills explains it this way: "Mandatory policies turn professionals away from women in abusive relationships by focusing so exclusively on arrest and prosecution and ignoring the opportunity, through human contact, to nurture a relationship with the victims." In short, mandatory arrest and prosecution policies silence women's voices.

And sometimes no-drop policies turn out to be embarrassing to all parties concerned:

> Former NFL quarterback Warren Moon got into an argument with his wife, Felicia. The police were summoned and, against her wishes, Mr. Moon was arrested. When the case went to trial, Felicia Moon admitted that she had instigated the altercation by kneeing him in the groin and throwing a candlestick at him Mr. Moon was acquitted of all charges.

Lulled into a False Sense of Security

American taxpayers pay hundreds of millions of dollars each year for domestic violence treatment programs and law enforcement and prosecution policies. Yet there is considerable doubt about the effectiveness of these programs.

Treatment: Offenders are often ordered to undergo treatment programs based on the Duluth model. But psychologist Donald Dutton, PhD notes, "Research shows that Duluth-oriented treatments are absolutely ineffective, and have no discernible impact on rates of recidivism." The National Research Council explains that these programs lack effectiveness because they are "driven by ideology and stakeholder interests rather than by plausible theories and scientific evidence of cause."

No-Drop Prosecution: Only one randomized study has been conducted that evaluates the effectiveness of no-drop prosecution. The research found that only one factor reduced abuser recidivism rates—allowing the victim to select whether and how aggressively the prosecutor would pursue the case. But by their nature, no-drop prosecution policies *eliminate* the ability of abused women to make that choice.

Restraining Orders: Restraining orders do not appear to be effective in deterring subsequent physical violence. One study [by J. Grau, J. Fagan, and S. Wexler] concluded that restraining orders were flatly "ineffective in stopping physical violence." Similarly a second report [by A. Harrell and B. Smith] concluded that "having a permanent order did not appear to deter most types of abuse." One review [by the Independent Women's Forum] concluded that such interventions may, in fact, "lull women into a false sense security."

Rigid Law Enforcement Programs Ensnare Women

The Violence Against Women Act encourages states to enact get-tough laws that promote the issuance of restraining orders, promote arrest, and facilitate prosecution efforts. But these laws may be going too far.

Restraining Orders: State laws have been broadened to the point that almost any action can be viewed as domestic "violence." Once a restraining order is in place, a vast range of ordinarily legal behavior becomes criminalized. As a result of open-ended definitions, almost any lover's quarrel or marital spat now qualifies as domestic abuse. Two to three million temporary restraining orders are currently issued each year— 15% of them against women, and many of them for trivial incidents:

> In August 2006, *Saturday Night Live* comedian Joe Piscopo obtained a restraining order against his wife, Kimberly. The allegation? She was using foul language and spitting at him.

Arrest: Thirty states have now enacted laws that promote or mandate arrest for domestic violence. As a result, the number of female offenders in domestic violence arrests rose by 10–25% in many areas. In California, the number of women arrested soared by 446% as a result of mandatory arrest policies, even though a number of those arrests may have been considered unnecessary by the woman's partner.

Prosecution: In Colorado, a "Fast Track" prosecution system put accused persons in jail, charged them with third-degree assault, and then offered a plea bargain involving a lesser charge. In exchange, the defendant agreed to not seek legal representation—a transparent violation of due process protections. One woman who went through the system stated, "It ain't about justice, that's for sure."

Female Abusers Can't Get the Help They Need

Research shows that women are at least as likely as men to engage in partner aggression. This is one example:

> On November 10, 2006, Krystle McGlothin of Peoria County, Illinois, rammed the pick-up truck of her ex-husband, Dennis, smashed its windows, and then ran him down, all the while yelling obscenities. Ms. McGlothin was charged with six counts of first-degree murder.

Most abusive women do not take their anger to the point of killing their partners. But where can violent women get the help they need?

Violence initiated by a woman increases the chances of retaliatory aggression *against* that woman. But experience reveals that when abusive women request help from VAWA-funded agencies, they learn that female-specific treatment programs are almost non-existent, and their requests for treatment may be dismissed with comments such as, "I'm sure you're under stress," or "He must have provoked you." Or if these women do find services designed specifically for women, they may find that female *offenders* are actually treated as the *victims*, which allows the abuse to continue.

Researcher Susan Steinmetz tells of receiving letters from violent women who recognized that they needed help, but were "turned away or being offered no help when they called a crisis line or shelter." As attorney Linda Kelly puts it, "Today's treatment denies the possibility that women can be violent."

When government policies neglect the problem, it's often children who pay the price:

> Socorro Caro of San Fernando Valley, California, had re-
> peatedly attacked her husband. But her husband, a well-
> known physician, was reluctant to report the incidents be-
> cause he thought that the authorities wouldn't believe him.
> On November 22, 1999, Mrs. Caro shot their three sons
> with a .38-caliber handgun. Two years later she was con-
> victed of first-degree murder.

Abuse Shelters Do Not Meet Victims' Needs

Abuse shelters are considered to be a mainstay of treatment services for domestic violence victims. But evidence support-ing the effectiveness of these shelters is not persuasive. Whether the outcome measure is recurrence of the violence, long-term separation of the abuser and victim, or victim satis-faction, the results have been found to be mixed.

One survey of shelters found that half of them stressed feminist political activism over providing women with practi-cal solutions to their problems. An example of such bias came from a former volunteer who was told by her supervisor to not advise an abused woman to learn self-defense techniques. Why? Because such advice could be interpreted as blaming the woman for not protecting herself.

In Massachusetts, one mother was pressured to attend a group for abused women run by volunteers with no profes-sional qualifications. She claimed that the clients were coerced by use of "threats, intimidation, and fear of losing their chil-dren." In the end, she filed a lawsuit against the shelter alleg-ing a variety of civil rights violations.

One recent investigation of abuse shelters uncovered a va-riety of illegal operations, including drug dealing. In one facility, staffers arranged for clients to provide sexual favors to law enforcement officers in exchange for the officers' false testimony in court. In another case, shelter residents were making money on the side working for a local call-girl service.

System Removes Children from Their Homes

In many states, the definition of child abuse has now been expanded so if a child simply *observes* partner aggression, it is deemed to constitute child abuse. The mere accusation of partner aggression means that that parent will also be suspected of child abuse—and the other parent may be charged with child neglect. That becomes grounds for removing the child from the family home.

In one case, a shelter held meetings for abused women and promised their statements would be kept confidential. In spite of assurances to the contrary, however, one woman's comments were passed along to the state child abuse agency. Shortly afterwards, the agency ordered the woman's daughter be removed from the home, accusing the mother of neglectfully allowing the girl to be exposed to domestic violence. The daughter, who had never suffered any physical abuse, was returned home 13 months later.

This is another example [as written by Glenn Sacks]:

A couple had several heated arguments, but neither had suffered any physical abuse. When Susan began to think about striking her husband with an object, she realized that she needed to get help. So she went to her local shelter to seek counseling. The shelter called the police to take a statement. The police report stated—erroneously—that Susan's husband had threatened to rape her and to kill the children.

On the basis of that faulty report, the husband was arrested and bail set at $350,000. He was eventually placed on 3 years probation. The children were placed in foster care for

38 days. The woman concluded, "These people have no idea of the damage they have done. I compare it to someone coming into your home and ransacking it."

In addition, when a restraining order is issued, it forbids contact not only between the alleged offender and the *victim*, but also between the alleged abuser and the *children*. This restriction extends to the couple's parents and extended family members as well. As a result, grandmothers and grandfathers may be prohibited from seeing their own grandchildren.

Policies Break Up Families and Harm Children

Research shows that the safest place for women is in the intact family. According to the Department of Justice, only 2% of partner aggression involves currently married couples who live together. The majority of domestic abuse incidents are minor, such as a shove or one-time slap. In such cases, reconciliation is preferable. But no-contact restraining orders and policies of women's shelters preclude persons from receiving couples' counseling.

Harvard law professor Jeannie Suk argues that restraining orders amount to "state-imposed *de facto* divorce" in which the mere presence of the accused offender in the family home becomes a proxy for the crime of domestic violence. As a result, the government "initiates and dictates the end of the intimate relationship as a solution to DV [domestic violence]." Suk wonders whether such orders violate persons' fundamental right to marry.

Some VAWA-funded programs appear to actively promote divorce. Abuse shelters have been referred to as "one-stop divorce shops." The website of one DoJ [Department of Justice]-funded program includes an advertisement for a divorce lawyer matching service.

Thus, a mere allegation of domestic violence—substantiated or not—can lead to family break-up. As a result, the child often loses regular contact with his or her non-custodial parent. Research shows that children who grow up in a one-parent family are at greater risk of child abuse, and fare worse on a broad range of indicators of academic, emotional, and social well-being. . . .

A Time for Reform

This Special Report reveals how the Violence Against Women Act—and the state-level laws it has engendered—are ineffective in reducing abuse, may place women at greater risk of violence, make it difficult for real victims to get help, ignore the wishes of abused women, lull women into a false sense of security, ensnare women in a rigid law enforcement bureaucracy, neglect the needs of female aggressors, fail to provide needed services at abuse shelters, remove kids from their homes, and harm families and children.

Previous Special Reports have documented other problems with VAWA, including discrimination against male victims, politicization of the judiciary, and violations of due process and civil rights.

Scientific research, expert panels, and individual cases all point to a singular conclusion: Our nation's domestic violence system, once conceived with high hopes and the best of intentions, is now in need of an overhaul.

It's time to reform the Violence Against Women Act.

Existing Batterer Intervention Programs Have Little Effect

National Institute of Justice

The National Institute of Justice is the law enforcement arm of the U.S. Department of Justice, Office of Justice Programs.

B atterer intervention programs have been proliferating in the United States [since the 1980s]. These programs give batterers an alternative to jail. They usually involve several months of attendance at group therapy sessions that attempt to stop the violence and change the batterers' attitudes toward women and battering.

Mounting evidence indicates that the programs might be ineffective.

Two recent evaluations, one in Broward County, Florida, and the other in Brooklyn, New York, evaluated interventions based on the Duluth model, which is the most commonly used program in the nation—many States mandate its use. The Broward County study found that the batterer intervention program had little or no effect, and the Brooklyn study found only minor improvement in some subjects. Neither program changed subjects' attitudes toward domestic abuse.

However, limitations in the studies raise additional issues. Are the evaluations correct that these programs don't change batterers' behavior and attitudes, or do shortcomings in the evaluations cover up program effects? There is no adequate answer to this question. Both issues may need to be addressed in future programs and studies.

The Findings in Broward County

The Broward County study found no significant difference between the treatment and control groups in attitudes toward

National Institute of Justice, *Do Batterer Intervention Programs Work? Two Studies*, Washington, DC: U.S. Department of Justice, Office of Justice Programs, September 2003.

the role of women, whether wife beating should be a crime, or whether the State has the right to intervene in cases of domestic violence. It also found no significant difference between these groups in whether victims expected their partners to beat them again. Moreover, no significant difference was found in violations of probation or rearrests, except that men who were assigned to the program but did not attend all sessions were more likely to be rearrested than members of the control group.

Evaluators tried to determine what could account for differences in men's self-reports of physical violence. They considered whether the offender was assigned to treatment; the number of classes he attended; and such stake-in-conformity variables [the elements of a person's life that make him or her more likely to conform to social norms] as marital status, residential stability, and employment. These last factors proved crucial.

Attending the program had no effect on the incidence of physical violence. Rather, offenders who were employed, married, and/or owned a home were less likely to batter again. Younger men and men with no stable residence (regardless of age) were more likely to abuse their partners. Older men who owned a home were less likely to do so.

Men who attended the longer treatment committed fewer new violent acts than those who attended the shorter treatment or those who had no treatment.

Twenty-four percent of men in both the experimental and control groups were rearrested at least once during their year on probation. Again, attending the program had no effect. Rather, whether an offender was employed (a stake-in-conformity variable) seemed to have more influence on whether he was rearrested.

The Findings in Brooklyn

The Brooklyn study unintentionally had two experimental groups of offenders. After the study was underway, defense attorneys objected to the 26-week program's duration and cost and advised their clients not to participate. To preserve the study, offenders were offered an accelerated 8-week program, which created a second experimental sample.

Batterers assigned to 26 weeks of treatment were less likely than the control group and those assigned to 8-week classes to be arrested again for a crime against the same victim. Neither program changed batterers' attitudes toward domestic violence. There were significant differences in reoffending, however. Even though more offenders completed the shorter program, the 26-week group had fewer criminal complaints than either the control group or the 8-week group.

Men who attended the longer treatment committed fewer new violent acts than those who attended the shorter treatment or those who had no treatment. This may suggest that providing treatment for a longer period of time helped reduce battering during the term of treatment and for some time thereafter.

Program and Research Issues

Concerns about research methodology cloud most batterer intervention program evaluations, and these two studies were no exception. The major issues are—

Maintaining sample integrity. Keeping assignments to batterer programs truly random is consistently a challenge.

Low attendance, high attrition, difficulty following up. High dropout and low response rates can lead to overly positive estimates of program effects.

Inadequate data sources. Official records used to validate batterer and victim reports may be collected inconsistently across jurisdictions; also, they capture only those violations that reach the authorities. Evidence suggests that batterers often avoid rearrest by switching to psychological and verbal abuse.

Difficulty measuring outcomes. Evaluators lack good survey instruments to measure batterer behavior and attitudes. The revised Conflict Tactics Scale (CTS2) used in these studies was not designed for before and after measurements. The Brooklyn study raised another issue common to batterer intervention program studies: Do evaluations examine the effects of the intervention or the effects of assignment to a treatment group?

Who is defining success? A final concern is broader in scope: Is a mere reduction in violence enough? These studies considered a reduction in violence to be a success based on the premise that it is unrealistic to expect batterers to abandon violent behavior after one intervention. But a "statistically significant reduction in violence" may mean little to a battered woman.

New Directions for Protecting Victims

The bottom line is: What are the best ways to protect victims? Batterer intervention programs are one approach, although much remains to be learned about them—specifically, which program works best for which batterer under which circumstances. But perhaps what is needed is a whole new approach.

Rethinking intervention. The models that underlie batterer intervention programs may need improvement. New approaches based on research into the causes of battering and batterer profiles may be more productive than a one-size-fits-all approach. Researchers may also draw lessons from other disciplines, such as substance abuse interventions—for example, that length of treatment may influence the outcome.

Improvements in how programs are put into practice may also be necessary, since variations in how programs are carried out may reduce their effectiveness. Researchers have noted greater effects in demonstration programs implemented by researchers than in practical programs implemented by juvenile or criminal justice agencies. Thus, the degree to which a program is faithful to the intervention model may determine how well it works. For example, some programs have few sanctions for dropping out, whereas others closely monitor attendance. This suggests the need to test the effectiveness of close monitoring and required attendance.

By collaborating, researchers, practitioners, and policymakers may be able to develop better strategies and improve the rigor of experimental evaluations.

Linking batterer programs to other programs and responses. Batterer intervention programs may be effective only in the context of a broader criminal justice and community response to domestic violence that includes arrest, restraining orders, intensive monitoring of batterers, and changes to social norms that inadvertently tolerate partner violence.

If monitoring is partly responsible for lower reoffense rates, as the Brooklyn experiment suggests, judicial monitoring may be a useful approach. The Judicial Oversight Demonstration initiative—a collaboration among the National Institute of Justice, the Office on Violence Against Women, and three local jurisdictions—is testing this idea. Other innovations might include mandatory intervention (indeterminate probation) until the batterer no longer endangers his partner, an approach that has been used with sex offenders.

Improving evaluations. Although the quality of batterer intervention program evaluations has improved, barriers remain. By collaborating, researchers, practitioners, and policymakers may be able to develop better strategies and improve the rigor of experimental evaluations.

For example, researchers need to find better ways to maintain contact with batterers and victims and better instruments than the revised CTS2. They need to develop more reliable ways of validating batterer and victim reports than relying strictly on official records of rearrests and probation violations. Statistical tools can be applied to correct for nonrandom assignment and other problems.

Since batterer intervention programs are a relatively new response to a critical social problem, it is too early to abandon the concept. More work needs to be done to determine the causes of battering and test new responses.

Law Enforcement Attitudes Have Hindered Efforts to Prevent and End Domestic Violence

Sara Catania

Sara Catania is a Los Angeles-based writer who has worked as a reporter with the Los Angeles Times *and the* LA Daily News. *She has reported extensively on criminal and social justice issues.*

On a warm day in 2001, Patty Prickett sat in her office in the West Los Angeles police station, trying not to cry. With her were a five-year-old boy and his younger sister, a week shy of her fourth birthday. The children did not know yet that their mother was dead. Six months earlier the woman had come to the station seeking safety. Her husband, she said, was unemployed and had been drinking heavily. When she refused to have sex with him he had attacked her, prevented her from calling for help, and held her captive in their home, blocking the bedroom doorway when she tried to flee.

Prickett, then head of the domestic abuse response team at the station, had accompanied the woman to court to secure a restraining order and advised her to quit her job, pull the children out of school, and leave home. The woman agreed, and Prickett located a scarce spot for the family in a shelter. "That is a very hard thing for a woman to do," she says. "To go into hiding while her batterer is running around free."

The woman was grateful for a respite from the constant threat of violence. But cut off from work and the emotional support of family and friends, she and the children soon became depressed. They left to stay at a relative's, where her husband quickly found her. She moved repeatedly, but he always tracked her down. Over the next six months her husband violated the court order many times—the woman filed at least six police reports recounting escalating incidents of death threats, stalking, and harassment. Prickett pressed the police and the Los Angeles city attorney's office to take action. Nothing happened. "One day he came and got her," Prickett says. "The kids saw them leave." Later that day the woman was found strangled to death with a belt. "She did everything right and the system wouldn't protect her," says Prickett. "They just wouldn't take it seriously. He kept saying he was going to kill her, and by God he did."

The question before the Court was what action, if any, the police are obligated to take when confronted with the violation of a restraining order.

Struggling Against the System

The murder that confronted Prickett in 2001 bears an eerie resemblance to the crime at the heart of *Castle Rock v. Gonzales*, a bellwether domestic violence case recently considered by the U.S. Supreme Court. In that case, a husband abducted three children from his estranged wife's custody, but when his wife, who had obtained a protection order for herself and the children, alerted police, they repeatedly put her off, telling her to call back later. That night the husband arrived at the police station and opened fire. He was shot and killed by police, who then discovered the children, dead in his truck. The question before the Court was what action, if any, the police are obligated to take when confronted with the violation of a restraining order. Every state now provides such civil protection orders to victims of domestic violence, and they are considered a basic tool in shielding victims from their batterers. But in both the West Los Angeles murder and the case before the Supreme Court, as well as in numerous cases across the country each year, the orders fail to fulfill their promise, and victims are subjected to harassment, beatings, and death.

What began as a scrappy, grassroots effort has become a bureaucratized entity allied so closely with the criminal justice system that it has sacrificed much of its ability to effectively critique that system and push for reform.

For Prickett, the 2001 murder in West Los Angeles marked the nadir of her career as an advocate. For 15 years she has been on the front lines of the battle against domestic violence, counseling both batterers and victims, fighting to find funding for programs that lock up abusers and keep victims safe, and growing increasingly frustrated with a legal system ill-equipped to handle the problem's complexity. Over the years she has shifted her focus several times, in each instance retrenching from burnout and from an approach she felt wasn't working. Her trajectory parallels that of the battered women's movement, as the euphoria of identifying a seemingly simple goal of safety succumbed to the realization that neither the end, nor the means of achieving it, was going to be easy. "The whole battered women's movement is set up to get women to leave their abusers," she says. "When they leave, we tell them we'll protect them, so what happens when we don't?"

Changes in the Domestic Violence Movement

Each year between 1 and 4 million women in the United States are victims of domestic violence, and 31 percent of women slain in this country are murdered by husbands, boyfriends, or exes—the majority killed after attempting to leave an abusive relationship. The fact that such statistics are routinely compiled and readily available is a testament to the mainstreaming of an issue that was barely acknowledged in the popular consciousness three decades ago. Since the 1970s, when domestic violence activism first emerged as an out-growth of the women's movement, proponents have won dramatic changes in policy, leaps in social awareness, and major infusions of cash from state and federal government.

But sustained institutional change requires vigilance, and the police indifference that greeted the murder in West Los Angeles illustrates a larger flaw in the evolution of the movement itself. What began as a scrappy, grassroots effort has become a bureaucratized entity allied so closely with the criminal justice system that it has sacrificed much of its ability to effectively critique that system and push for reform. "Twenty-five years ago we had a notion that we were organizing to change the system," says Ellen Pence, a founder of the Domestic Abuse Intervention Project in Duluth, Minnesota, a leader of the national movement. "Then this funny change happened, where instead of us advocating for what women needed from the system, we started advocating the system to women. There has to be a new confrontation of what's going on."

Prickett believes that lack of confrontation, and of any larger consequence for police inaction, enabled officers to brush off her warnings about the homicidal batterer in 2001. "What they will say, what they always say, is you never know which ones are going to wind up killing someone," she says. "But there are signs, and once you see them, you have to act, and you have to be aggressive. Otherwise women are going to keep on getting hurt and getting killed." After the woman's death, Prickett heard that the husband had been seen hanging out at a bar near the scene of the crime. She begged the cops to stake it out. They refused. He was never apprehended.

Resistance from Law Enforcement

The West Los Angeles police station guards a geographically and economically diverse region spanning 65 square miles, encompassing no-frills apartment complexes and some of the most affluent addresses in the city, like Pacific Palisades and

Brentwood, the neighborhood where Nicole Brown Simpson was murdered in 1994. The precinct boasts the lowest crime rate in the city and, partly as a result, officers and advocates say, the station is resistant to change. "People here think they're doing just fine," says Rashad Sharif, a senior lead officer at the station and a friend of Prickett's. "They say, 'If it ain't broke, don't fix it.'"

Prickett set up shop at the police station in 1998 under a four-year, $540,000 program funded by the Violence Against Women Act. That landmark legislation, passed by Congress in 1994, provides essential funding for hundreds of criminal justice programs that now undergird battered women's advocacy nationwide. Prickett's program was intended to educate officers, help victims get access to services, and increase arrests and prosecutions of batterers. Though the funding was awarded to the police department, Prickett came in as an advocate, a stance that fueled an adversarial dynamic between her and a station considered within the local advocacy community as one of many mired in a "good old boy" culture.

Prickett confronted the station's disregard the day she reported to work and was shown to her office—a former holding cell, complete with iron bars and a concrete floor. A detective told her dismissively that "rich men don't beat their wives." Undeterred, Prickett sponge-painted the walls peach, carpeted the floor with remnants, and tacked up posters of Sojourner Truth and Rosa Parks. On the weekends when she went to political protests, she made a point of hugging any police officers she recognized. "They never quite knew what to make of that," she says, laughing. "But I wanted them to see things from a different perspective, to see the crowd as people."

At the station, she and her staff of five held marathon training sessions on rape, on determining the dominant aggressor in domestic violence situations where both individuals are injured, and on writing effective reports, crucial because "the chances of getting a victim to testify are slim to none," she says. "That initial report has to be of detective caliber so that it can stand alone in the prosecution."

Prickett wrote manuals for the officers, passed out pocket-size how-to-identify-a-batterer guides, and went out on more than a thousand domestic violence calls. She or one of her staff members was on duty, in a police car accompanied by officers, from 6 p.m. to 2 a.m. five nights a week. "When I first started, the last thing I wanted was to be part of a responder team," she says. "I mean, 2 a.m. in a black-and-white? Give me a break. But as time went on I realized that was the way to go. You can really intervene and help the woman get hooked up to services before she gets spooked."

Multiple studies have found that when a coordinated model is properly applied, domestic violence-related homicides and felony assaults fall by as much as half.

Whatever Prickett's success in the field, her suggestions back at the station fell on deaf ears. "Everything I would write up, they would sort of laugh at me and pat me on the head and tell me why we couldn't do it," she says. "I was like, 'What do you mean we can't do it? Fresno P.D. is doing it.' They'd say, 'Well, we just don't do that.'"

Michael Hillmann, a captain in West L.A. during part of Prickett's tenure, says the station was supportive of the program, but that domestic violence calls often lose out to more pressing crimes. "In the grander scheme of things, reduction of homicides and the ability to save the lives of people subject to drive-bys is a competing priority," says Hillmann, now a deputy chief supervising drug and gang operations. "We're trying to balance all that. To take police officers out of the field and put them with a domestic violence program means that we have one less officer in a position where they are able to prevent a shooting or some other type of crime."

Modest Gains Offset by Resentment and Apathy

Multiple studies have found that when a coordinated model is properly applied, domestic violence-related homicides and felony assaults fall by as much as half. "I don't think the criminal justice system can get rid of wife-beating," says Pence. "But if everyone is very aggressive and very consistent, it makes an enormous difference." Yet sustained results have proved elusive. In 1977, Los Angeles became one of the first cities in the country to establish a separate domestic violence unit and adopt a vertical prosecution model, boosting their success rate by assigning each case to a single attorney from beginning to end. Even with those innovations, says Maureen Siegel, special counsel in the criminal division for the Los Angeles city attorney's office, her office accepts for prosecution only about a third of the domestic violence cases that come in. "No matter how strongly we may believe an incident has occurred," Siegel says, "knowing something and being able to prove it in court are, unfortunately, two very different things."

Advocates say the time has come for the movement to address the burgeoning resistance associated with the men's rights movement, the legal challenges being mounted on behalf of batterers by the defense bar, and entrenched resentment and apathy within the criminal justice system itself.

Peter Macdonald, a retired judge from Kentucky who leads judicial domestic violence training programs, says judges tend to come under the sway of batterers who appear charming and polished, while victims are intimidated into recanting or are made to look hysterical. "This happens all the time," Macdonald says. "I'm embarrassed to say that when I started out in 1978, I was one of those judges." Some judges have never heard of the Violence Against Women Act, Macdonald says, and are ignorant of changes in the law affecting battered women. At one training session he conducted, he says, only 1 of 47 participating judges knew that a protection order issued in one state is valid in every other.

Yet ignorance is no longer the main enemy. "Twenty years ago we could say nobody understood domestic violence and we have a lot to educate them about," says Joan Meier, a professor of clinical law at George Washington University. "Well, we've done that. People understand it a lot better now. Now we face a much more difficult challenge, because the resistance is much more deep and fundamental and bedrock." Advocates say the time has come for the movement to address the burgeoning resistance associated with the men's rights movement, the legal challenges being mounted on behalf of batterers by the defense bar, and entrenched resentment and apathy within the criminal justice system itself.

"There's a huge backlash right now," says Susan Millmann, a legal aid attorney who heads the L.A. Domestic Violence Task Force. "There are many, many people who are trying to turn back the clock." Millmann finds Prickett's experience in West Los Angeles unsurprising. There, as in many police stations around the country, line officers have little incentive to embrace an effective approach without a push from the top. "The officers say what they're supposed to say," Prickett says. "That is, 'You don't decide whether to prosecute, ma'am, the state prosecutes.' And then they put some detective on the phone. We had one guy who spent more time talking victims out of prosecuting, which is totally against policy. But as a civilian, you can show L.A.P.D. their own penal code and their own policy manual and it doesn't matter unless you've got backing from the captain. Somebody has to care."

The Background of the Domestic Violence Movement

Patricia Prickett, who is 58, divorced, and the mother of two grown sons, never imagined she'd wind up as an advocate for battered women. She came of age in the 1960s and 1970s, dividing her energies among the antiwar movement, the environment, and lefty political campaigns. Her manner is both direct and disarming, and she frequently employs a mischievous humor that challenges social taboos—at one point she and some friends started a group called Tough Women Against Toxics, wearing T-shirts with the acronym on prominent display. "We'd go to nice parties and watch people's responses," she says with a raspy smoker's laugh. "They'd start off like, 'Oh that's great,' and then they'd be like, 'Oh. . . . Oh. . . . Oh.' And then they'd run away."

Meanwhile, domestic violence was gaining ground with women's rights activists and in the courts, especially after a 1978 New York court case, *Bruno v. Codd*, in which 12 battered women seeking damages for inadequate police response provided affidavits detailing gruesome accounts of abuse. The court sympathized with the women and expressed dissatisfaction with the police. "It was the first judicial airing of what was wrong with the way society responds to battered women, and how out of date it is," says Meier, who is director of the Domestic Violence Legal Empowerment and Appeals Project. "It was very powerful in bringing the truth to light."

In 1984, more than 200 battered women created the Power and Control Wheel, a diagnostic tool describing abusive behavior patterns.

For the next decade, the movement continued to grow, manifested mostly by the emergency shelters and hot lines that were established. In 1983, the problem entered the mainstream when *Time* featured a graphic cover photo of a battered woman. "That was a measure of where we were then," Meier says. "It wasn't talked about, and it wasn't understood. All of us who were interested in the field went and snatched up all the copies."

It was around that time that Prickett, weary of the constant hustle of activism, changed course. Her father had been a Marine and had spent three and a half years in a Japanese prison camp during World War II. He didn't talk much about his ordeal, but what he did describe—being kept immobile in a hole for a month, eating raw flour until he threw up—moved and disturbed her. "I was always interested in the concept of abuse of power," she says. "I felt like it was time to take that on."

She went back to school for a master's in clinical psychology, intending to become a marriage and family therapist. Mindful of her father's experience, she sought out course work on abuse, which in a family setting included domestic violence. What she found dismayed her. The only related writing focused on sexual abuse, and it placed the blame squarely on the victim.

Working with Batterers

Beyond the confines of the classroom, the social landscape was changing. In 1984, more than 200 battered women created the Power and Control Wheel, a diagnostic tool describing abusive behavior patterns. The wheel has since become the talisman of the therapeutic model for addressing domestic violence and is still widely applied. Domestic violence had also gained enough recognition that courts began ordering counseling for abusers, and Prickett found an internship at a community clinic in Los Angeles that ran such a group. "The batterer thing appealed to me partly because at the time nobody else wanted to do it," she says. "And I was attracted to the idea that if you could do good work with them you would have an impact on a lot of people, as opposed to working with survivors, where it's one at a time."

Batterers' groups were seen as the humane antidote to abusive behavior. But a series of studies called into question whether they actually altered the way men viewed their actions enough to prevent them from repeating the abuse. In 1984, a study conducted by the Minneapolis Domestic Violence Experiment found that batterers are half as likely to commit repeat violence within six months if they serve jail time. In 1987, in a landmark case called *Thurman v. City of Torrington*, a federal district court awarded a battered wife $2.3 million after police refused to arrest her husband. This case, along with the Minneapolis study, spurred a wave of tough arrest laws around the country, begetting an uneasy alliance between the battered women's movement and the traditional advocates of law and order.

At first, Prickett believed that counseling alone might work. Eventually she, too, concluded that it could be effective only if men attended for several years—in conjunction with jail time. "There has to be desire for change on the part of the batterer," she says. "That's why jail works. Sometimes the only desire is to stay out of jail."

From the day I walked in the door I fought the same battles, over and over and over again. Nothing changed.

Raising the Profile of Domestic Violence

While Prickett immersed herself in batterers' counseling, O.J. Simpson, an alumnus of court-mandated counseling programs, went on trial for the murder of his ex-wife, Nicole Brown Simpson. The trial achieved what 20 years of activism had not, legitimizing battering as a crime category and persuading millions of Americans that domestic violence was not solely an issue for the poor and drug-addled. Lynn Rosenthal, director of the National Network to End Domestic Violence, was running a shelter at the time. By 1995, the year of the trial, calls for help had soared by 40 percent. "The O.J. case changed our work forever," Rosenthal says. "We had to rush to keep up, and we're still catching up."

The year before, Congress passed the Violence Against Women Act. Many states enacted civil protection orders and mandatory arrest laws, requiring cops to arrest batterers even against the wishes of the victim. To further protect against victim intimidation, cities adopted no-drop policies; prosecution would continue even if a woman backed out.

Those changes led to a dramatic uptick in attention to domestic violence within the criminal justice system, and in 1996, at a training session at the Los Angeles Police Academy, Prickett heard a former sheriff's deputy speak about being beaten by a boyfriend, an L.A.P.D. officer. Thanks to new federal and state funding, the woman told the crowd, anti-battering programs could educate the police by partnering with them. For the first time in a long while, Prickett felt inspired. "I thought, 'I want to work with her; I want to do what she's doing.'" The following year she reported for work at the police station in West Los Angeles to begin her second chapter as an advocate in the battered women's movement, this time with a focus on enforcement instead of counseling. That chapter would end in disillusionment, when the 2001 murder indicated to her that her efforts were futile. "Four years sitting in a cell," she says. "From the day I walked in the door I fought the same battles, over and over and over again. Nothing changed." In mid-2002, when the funding for Prickett's program ran out, the station declined to seek a renewal.

Focusing on Helping One Victim at a Time

Three years later, Prickett paid a visit to the precinct house and saw little evidence of her tenure. Her "cell" had been converted into normal office space—a microwave sat in the spot that had been the intake desk for sex offenders. There were no domestic violence posters in the lobby, just a few pamphlets stacked alongside brochures on Halloween safety and real estate fraud. And more importantly, there was no longer specialized training for officers, and no volunteers to accompany them on domestic violence calls.

"While Patty was here it got people talking about domestic violence," says Officer Rashad Sharif. "Maybe they cared, maybe they didn't. But at least they were aware of the issue and they had been trained on how to handle it. Now it's back to just the basics, whatever they get at the academy, which is more than what they offered when I was there, but it's still not at the level of robbery, rape, and drugs. It's still on the fringe."

The longer I do this, the more I'm reminded that domestic violence is everybody's problem.

After the West Los Angeles experiment, Prickett lost some of her enthusiasm for laboring in a confrontational environment. "It's hard to work in a place where people are happy when there's an execution," she says. "It's exhausting." As a member of the city's Domestic Violence Task Force, she tried to secure funding for a range of programs. She revived her private practice, taking on victims of domestic violence, and also became a counselor in the health clinic at Manual Arts High School, one of the most dangerous and academically underperforming high schools in the city, thinking the position would provide a break from battered women's advocacy. Instead, she's been confronted with the issue yet again. "These kids see violence every day," she says. "They see shootings and all kinds of brutality, in the streets and in the home."

Once again, Prickett's transition reflects the evolution in the battered women's movement, which is broadening beyond the current focus on cops and courts to include social services like the kind Prickett is providing at Manual Arts. Outside her office at the high school on a morning in mid-April, a dark-haired teen in baggy pants and a hooded sweatshirt stands waiting as Prickett approaches. They embrace in greeting, and she ushers him inside. More than half of the students she counsels at the school have witnessed domestic violence—a bad harbinger, considering that children who witness abuse are more likely to become perpetrators. Recent reports indicate that domestic violence in teen relationships is on the rise. Prickett's work with students is one small bulwark against that trend. "You just can't get away from it," she says. "The longer I do this, the more I'm reminded that domestic violence is everybody's problem."

Contrary to what she believed starting out, she has learned that helping one victim helps many—the woman, her children, and the relatives and the extended community affected by abuse. As Prickett aids the students, the students aid her. Through them, she has gained direct access to some of their victimized parents, whom she talks with on the phone, directs to services, and sometimes persuades to come in. In each ease she hopes she might do something, any small thing, to avoid a repetition of that day in 2001 when she sat in her police station office before two young, motherless children, and didn't know what to say.

Organizations to Contact

The editors have compiled the following list of organizations concerned with the issues debated in this book. The descriptions are derived from materials provided by the organizations. All have publications or information available for interested readers. The list was compiled on the date of publication of the present volume; names, addresses, and phone numbers may change. Be aware that many organizations take several weeks or longer to respond to inquiries, so allow as much time as possible.

American Bar Association Commission on Domestic Violence
740 15th St. NW, Washington, DC   20005-1019
(202) 662-1000
Web site: http://www.abanet.org/domviol

The American Bar Association's Commission on Domestic Violence provides ongoing education, publications, and technical assistance to attorneys representing domestic violence and sexual assault victims.

Child Welfare Information Gateway
Children's Bureau/ACYF, Washington, DC   20024
(703) 385-7565
Web site: http://www.childwelfare.gov

The Child Welfare Information Gateway, which was formed by the merger of the National Clearinghouse on Child Abuse and Neglect Information and the National Adoption Information Clearinghouse, is run by the U.S. Department of Health and Human Service's Children's Bureau in the Administration for Children and Families. The Gateway publishes reports and information on child abuse statistics, healthy families, fathers' rights, and safe haven laws.

Childhelp
15757 N. 78th St., Scottsdale, AZ   85260
(480) 922-8212 • Fax: (480) 922-7061
Web site: http://www.childhelp.org

Childhelp works to help prevent and treat child abuse. The organization provides residential care and counseling services for abused and neglected children through its group and foster homes. It promotes public awareness of child abuse issues and offers a child abuse hotline that services North America. Its publications include the book *Child Abuse and You* and the periodical *Child Help Newsletter*.

Emerge: Counseling and Education to Stop Domestic Violence
2464 Massachusetts Ave., Suite 101, Cambridge, MA   02140
(617) 547-9879 • Fax: (617) 547-0904
Web site: http://www.emergedv.com

Emerge works to prevent domestic violence by providing counseling services and training workshops for batterers, conducting research, and disseminating information and referrals for other services. The group offers parenting seminars for fathers, anger management courses for men, and batterer intervention training for therapists and counselors.

FaithTrust Institute
2400 N. 45th St., #101, Seattle, WA   98102
(206) 634-1903 • Fax: (206) 634-0115
Web site: http://www.faithtrustinstitute.org

FaithTrust Institute is an international, interfaith organization devoted to addressing the cultural and religious aspects of domestic and sexual violence. The group provides support and educational resources to religious organizations to encourage healthy family relationships and disperse information on sexual violence against women, children, and immigrants.

Family Research Laboratory (FRL)
University of New Hampshire, Durham, NH   03824-3586
(603) 862-1888 • Fax: (603) 862-1122
Web site: http://www.unh.edu/frl

Since 1975, Family Research Laboratory has devoted itself primarily to understanding the causes and consequences of family violence and working to dispel myths about family violence through public education. The organization publishes numerous books and articles on the physical abuse of children, the physical abuse of spouses or cohabitants, marital rape, corporal punishment, dating violence, pornography, and verbal aggression.

Family Violence Prevention Fund (FVPF)
383 Rhode Island St., Suite 304, San Francisco, CA   94103
(415) 252-8900 • Fax: (415) 252-8991
Web site: http://www.endabuse.org

Family Violence Prevention Fund is a national nonprofit organization concerned with domestic violence education, prevention, and public policy reform. It works to improve health care for battered women and to strengthen the judicial system's capacity to respond appropriately to domestic violence cases. The Fund publishes brochures, action kits, books, and general information packets on domestic violence.

Humane Society of the United States
2100 L St. NW, Washington, DC   20037
(202) 452-1100
Web site: http://www.hsus.org

The Humane Society of the United States instituted its First Strike campaign in 1997 to raise awareness of the documented connection between animal abuse and human violence, including violence within families, where pets often are victims. The First Strike campaign encourages cooperation among various law enforcement, social service, and animal control agencies, providing educational and legal support to family violence and animal welfare professionals.

Institute for Family Violence Studies

Florida State University, Tallahassee, FL 32306-2570
(850) 644-9596 • Fax: (850) 644-8331
Web site: http://familyvio.csw.fsu.edu

The Institute for Family Violence Studies conducts research on family violence and gender discrimination, provides training for industry professionals and advocates, and conducts online tutorials for the study of domestic violence issues.

National Coalition Against Domestic Violence (NCADV)

1120 Lincoln St., Suite 1603, Denver, CO 80203
(303) 839-1852 • Fax: (303) 831-9251
Web site: http://www.ncadv.org

NCADV was formed in 1978 and became the largest U.S. coalition of grassroots shelter programs and services for battered women and their children. The organization provides technical help and education to family violence professionals, advocates for public policy and legislation, and it sponsors national conferences that bring together the leading thinkers in family violence policy, law, and services.

National Coalition of Anti-Violence Programs (NCAVP)

240 West 35th St., New York, NY 10001
(212) 714-1184 • Fax: (212) 714-2627
Web site: http://www.ncavp.org

The National Coalition of Anti-Violence Programs is a nationwide network of organizations that address the problem of violence in and against the gay/lesbian/bisexual/transgendered/HIV-AIDS-afflicted community, including intimate partner violence (IPV). The group monitors IPV statistics and publishes periodic incidence reports.

National Committee for the Prevention of Elder Abuse (NCPEA)

1612 K Street NW, Suite 400, Washington, DC   20006
(202) 682-4140 • Fax: (202) 223-2099
Web site: http://www.preventelderabuse.org

The National Committee for the Prevention of Elder Abuse identifies the elderly as the most vulnerable people in our society, at risk for all manner of violence, including domestic and sexual abuse. The group conducts research, provides training, performs coalition-building at the state and local levels, and acts as a consultant for the development of a national Elder Justice Act. The organization also publishes the *Journal of Elder Abuse and Neglect.*

National Council of Juvenile and Family Court Judges (NCJFCJ)

PO Box 8970, Reno, NV   89507
(775) 784-6012 • Fax: (775) 784-6628
Web site: http://www.ncjfcj.org

The National Council of Juvenile and Family Court Judges offers juvenile-justice professionals information and technical assistance on a variety of topics, including child abuse and neglect, the foster care system, and custody disputes. The Council operates the Resource Center on Domestic Violence: Child Protection and Custody, a national resource center funded by the U.S. Department of Health and Human Services.

National Domestic Violence Hotline (NDVH)

1-800-799-SAFE (7233)
Web site: http://www.ndvh.org

The National Domestic Violence Hotline is an emergency hotline available throughout the United States, Puerto Rico, and the U.S. Virgin Islands to domestic violence victims and their families and friends, with advisers available twenty-four hours a day to help devise escape plans, provide referrals, and perform crisis intervention.

National Family Violence Legislative Resource Center

e-mail: info@nfvlrc.org
Web site: http://www.nfvlrc.org

The National Family Violence Legislative Resource Center is a Web-based gathering of researchers, advocates, educators, mental health professionals, and batterer intervention group leaders devoted to creating nonpartisan, nonideological, and gender-inclusive family violence legislation and public policy in the United States and Canada.

National Institute of Justice Violence Against Women and Family Violence Research and Evaluation Program

810 7th St. NW, Washington, DC   20531
NIJ Director's Office: (202) 307-6394
Web site: http://www.ojp.usdoj.gov

As an arm of the U.S. Department of Justice, the National Institute of Justice's Violence Against Women and Family Violence program exists to analyze and disseminate research on family violence in order to increase the effectiveness of criminal justice agencies' responses to the problem.

Sanctuary for Families

PO Box 1406, New York, NY   10268
(212) 349-6009 • Fax: (212) 349-6810
Web site: http://www.sanctuaryforfamilies.org

Sanctuary for Families approaches family violence as a violation of human rights and advocates for societal change to ensure the dignity of women and children. The group offers shelter, clinical, and legal services with a holistic approach that takes into account the cultural and language barriers that often prevent victims from seeking help.

Stop Family Violence

331 W. 57th St., #518, New York, NY   10019
Web site: http://www.stopfamilyviolence.org

Stop Family Violence was formed in 2000 in response to the near-expiration of the Violence Against Women Act. The group used the wide-reaching power of the Internet to organize 164,000 activists to petition Congress to reauthorize the legislation. Stop Family Violence continues to act as a clearinghouse for family violence-related news and pending legislation at the federal, state, and local levels.

Bibliography

Books

David Adams

Why Do They Kill? Men Who Murder Their Intimate Partners. Nashville: Vanderbilt University Press, 2007.

Lundy Bancroft

When Dad Hurts Mom: Helping Your Children Heal the Wounds of Witnessing Abuse. New York: G.P. Putnam's Sons, 2004.

Ola W. Barnett, Cindy Miller-Perrin, and Robin Perrin

Family Violence Across the Lifespan: An Introduction. 2nd ed. Thousand Oaks, CA: Sage Publications, 2004.

Richard J. Bonnie and Robert B. Wallace

Elder Mistreatment: Abuse, Neglect, and Exploitation in an Aging America. Washington, DC: National Academies Press, 2002.

Ricardo Carrillo and Jerry Tello, eds.

Family Violence and Men of Color: Healing the Wounded Male Spirit. 2nd ed. New York: Springer Publishing Company, 2008.

Christina Dalpiaz

Breaking Free, Starting Over: Parenting in the Aftermath of Family Violence. Westport, CT: Praeger, 2004.

Richard L. Davis

Domestic Violence: Intervention, Prevention, Policies, and Solutions. Boca Raton, FL: CRC Press, 2008.

Donald Dutton   *Rethinking Domestic Violence.*
                  Vancouver: University of British
                  Columbia Press, 2006.

Margaret M.   *Children Exposed to Violence.*
Feerick and   Baltimore: Paul H. Brookes
Gerald B.   Publishers, 2006.
Silverman, eds.

Barry Goldstein   *Scared to Leave, Afraid to Stay: Paths
                  from Family Violence to Safety.*
                  Bandon, OR: Robert D. Reed
                  Publishers, 2002.

J. Hamel and T.   *Family Approaches to Domestic
Nicholls, eds.   Violence: A Guide to Gender-Inclusive
                  Research and Treatment.* New York:
                  Springer Publishing Company, 2006.

Karel   *Violence in the Home:
Kurst-Swanger   Multidisciplinary Perspectives.* New
                  York: Oxford University Press, 2003.

Kathleen   *Family Violence in a Cultural
Malley-Morrison   Perspective: Defining, Understanding,
and Denise A.   and Combating Abuse.* Thousand
Hines   Oaks, CA: Sage Publications, 2003.

Linda G. Mills   *Insult to Injury: Rethinking Our
                  Responses to Intimate Abuse.*
                  Princeton, NJ: Princeton University
                  Press, 2003.

Audrey   *Children's Perspectives on Domestic
Mullender, Gill   Violence.* Thousand Oaks, CA: Sage
Hague, Umme F.   Publications, 2002.
Iman, et al.

Andrea Parrot *Forsaken Females: The Global*
and Nina *Brutalization of Women*. Lanham,
Cummings MD: Rowman and Littlefield
Publishers, 2006.

Janice L. Ristock *No More Secrets: Violence in Lesbian*
Relationships. New York: Routledge,
2002.

Periodicals

Phil Arkow "Expanding Domestic Violence
Protective Orders to Include
Companion Animals," American Bar
Association Commission on
Domestic Violence, *eNewsletter* 8,
Summer 2007.
http://www.abanet.org/
domviol/enewsletter/vol8/
expertArkow.html.

Emily Bazelon "Hitting Bottom: Why America
Should Outlaw Spanking," *Slate*,
January 25, 2007.
http://www.slate.com/id/2158310/.

Larry Bennett and "Controversies and Recent Studies of
Oliver Williams Batterer Intervention Program
Effectiveness," National Electronic
Network on Violence Against Women
(VAWnet), August 2001. http://new.
vawnet.org/category/Main_Doc.
php?docid=373.

Emma Bevan and   "Is Domestic Violence Learned? The
Daryl J. Higgins   Contribution of Five Forms of Child
Maltreatment to Men's Violence and
Adjustment," *Journal of Family
Violence* 17, no. 3, September 2002:
223–45.

Bonnie Brandl   "Domestic Abuse in Later Life,"
and Loree   Applied Research Forum, National
Cook-Daniels   Electronic Network on Violence
Against Women (VAWnet), December
2002. http://www.ncall.us/
docs/AR_later-life.pdf.

Doris Williams   "Intimate Partner Violence in African
Campbell, Phyllis   American Women," *The Online
Sharps, and Faye   Journal of Issues in Nursing* 7, no. 1,
Gary   January 2002.
http://www.nursingworld.org/
MainMenuCategories/ANAMarketplace/
ANAPeriodicals/OJIN.aspx.

Clifton P. Flynn   "Woman's Best Friend: Pet Abuse and
the Role of Companion Animals in
the Lives of Battered Women,"
Violence Against Women 6, no. 2,
February 2000: 162–77.

Amy   "Male Versus Female Intimate
Holtzman-Munroe   Partner Violence: Putting
Controversial Findings into Context,"
Journal of Marriage and Family 67,
December 2005: 1120–25.

Tom Jackman   "Woman Beaten by Husband Wins
Suit," *Washington Post*, August 18,
2006, B01.

Alan E. Kazdin   "Spare the Rod: Why You Shouldn't Hit Your Kids," *Slate*, September 24, 2008. http://www.slate.com/id/2200450/.

Christopher D. Maxwell, Joel H. Garner, and Jeffrey A. Fagan   "The Effects of Arrest on Intimate Partner Violence: New Evidence from the Spouse Assault Replication Program," *National Institute of Justice Research in Brief*, July 2001: 1–15.

Judith McFarlane, Ann Malecha, Julia Gist, et al.   "Protection Orders and Intimate Partner Violence: An 18-Month Study of 150 Black, Hispanic, and White Women," *American Journal of Public Health* 94, no. 4, April 2004: 613–18.

Vera E. Mouradian   "Battered Women: What Goes into the Stay-Leave Decision?," *Wellesley Centers for Women Research and Action Report*, Fall-Winter 2004: 34–35.

Karen S. Peterson   "Studies Shatter Myth About Abuse," *USA Today*, June 22, 2003. http://www.usatoday.com/news/health/2003-06-22-abuse-usat_x.htm.

Loretta Pyles   "Economic Well-Being and Intimate Partner Violence: New Findings about the Informal Economy," *Journal of Sociology and Social Welfare*, September 1, 2006.

Warren Richey — "Court Sides with Police in Restraining-Order Case," *Christian Science Monitor*, June 28, 2005. http://www.csmonitor.com/2005/0628/p23s01-usju.htm.

Linda E. Saltzman, Y.T. Green, J.S. Marks, et al. — "Violence Against Women as a Public Health Issue," *American Journal of Preventive Medicine* 19, no. 4, 2000: 325–29.

Melissa M. Stiles — "Witnessing Domestic Violence: The Effect on Children," *American Family Physician* 66, no. 11, December 1, 2002: 2052–65. http://www.aafp.org/afp/20021201/medicine.html.

UNICEF — "Domestic Violence Against Women and Girls," *Innocenti Digest*, no. 6, June 2000: 1–27.

Diana Wempen — "Four-Footed and Largely Forgotten: Exploring the Connections Between Animal Abuse and Domestic Violence," American Bar Association Commission on Domestic Violence, *eNewsletter* 8, Summer 2007. http://www.abanet.org/domviol/enewsletter/vol8/expertWempen.html.

Hallie Bongar White and Jane Larrington — "Intersection of Domestic Violence and Child Victimization in Indian Country," Southwest Center for Law and Policy/Office on Violence Against Women, U.S. Department of Justice, 2005.

Eilene
Zimmerman

"Spanking Mad," *Salon*, February 5, 2007. http://www.salon.com/mwt/feature/2007/02/05/spanking_bill/print.html.

Index

R